MW00416323

MEL BAY PRESENTS

DAVID GRISMAN   TONY RICE

TONE POEMS

TRANSCRIBED BY JOHN CARLINI

*T his project is dedicated
to all the nameless and faceless
artisans and craftsmen who built these
wonderful guitars and mandolins
that we love to play.*

Published in conjunction with:

ACOUSTIC DISC
100% HANDMADE MUSIC
™

Visit us on the Web at http://www.melbay.com — E-mail us at email@melbay.com

Vintage Voices

Great singers are born with their instruments; acoustic instrumentalists must choose them. How does one "select a voice"? As a novice bluegrass mandolinist in the early '60s, I began to emulate my musical heroes, Ralph Rinzler, Frank Wakefield, and of course, the great tonal practitioner, Bill Monroe. As I soon learned, they all played older Gibson F-5 models. Soon I was on my own path of tonal discovery, acquiring in succession a '60s Kay plywood pawn-shop special, a -'20s Gibson A-Junior, a 1919 Gibson F-4, a 1951 Gibson F-5, and finally, a 1924 Gibson Loar F-5. Each instrument cost a little more than its predecessor and took me a step closer to "my sound." As I progressed on this journey, I became increasingly enamored with the sounds of these instruments, each with its own subtle differences and potential. At that time, terms like "vintage," "Lloyd Loar," and "herringbone," were not associated with the instruments; they were simply "used" or "old." I certainly did not view them as investments, or stock shares that would soon be splitting. But I loved them, their tone, feel, smell (probably more due to their musty cases), and vibe. I still do, but now vintage guitars and mandolins are big business.

As the current market values for these instruments have expanded way beyond the means of the average contemporary acoustic musician, something sad (to me) has taken place; more of them are now owned by wealthy collectors, who have in effect taken them out of circulation. Many of them sit in closets and glass cases, unplayed and unheard. The focus has shifted from the music!

The purpose of this recording is to redirect some of the attention being paid to vintage guitars and mandolins back to their musical values.

What do they sound like? Is one of these instruments worth 10 times more than another, when it comes down to the music? To assist in this experiment, I invited my friend Tony Rice to lend his masterly touch to 17 vintage guitars, while I played 17 vintage mandolins. Dexter Johnson, a fine luthier and proprietor of the acoustic-only Carmel Music, helped us set up and select the instruments, and my expert engineer, David Dennison, recorded our duets, live to 2-track analog, without any tonal enhancement, using the same microphones and set-up for each cut. Here are the results, complete with some wonderful photographs by Eric Harger: a mini-reference on a subject that's been dear to my heart for over 30 years now.

– David Grisman, January 1994

Transcriptions of this landmark recording by John Carlini

Special thanks to Craig Miller for helping the process of getting this wonderful music in print.

William Bay

TONY RICE

Arguably the greatest living practitioner of the art of bluegrass flatpicking, Tony Rice is a Grammy award-winning acoustic guitarist whose world-famous tone made him the logical choice for this project.

In 1975, Tony became the original guitarist in the David Grisman Quintet, with which he helped to alter the course of American string band music.

After four years of touring and recording with David, Tony embarked on a solo career with his own "Tony Rice Unit" as well as numerous other recording projects such as the widely acclaimed "Bluegrass Album Band." Although he almost always performs and records with his legendary 1935 Martin D-28 (formerly owned by Clarence White), the companion recording displays Tony's complete mastery of tone production on an extremely wide range of instruments, including the current Santa Cruz model that bears his name.

DAVID GRISMAN

The tone of David Grisman's mandolin has graced hundreds of recordings and concert halls since the start of his career over 30 years ago. His stature as a bandleader is reflected by those artists who have played with his groups and on his recordings: Svend Assmussen, Hal Blaine, Vassar Clements, Stephanie Grappelli, Mark O'Connor, and of course, Tony Rice, to name a few. David has also been a record producer all these years with classic albums by Red Allen, Dave Apollon, Jethro Burns, Tiny Moore, "Old & in the Way," and Frank Wakefield. In 1990, David helped establish Acoustic Disc as a means of furthering his goals as a purveyor of acoustic music. As part of his continuing affection for the mandolin and its music, David has acquired an extensive collection of vintage mandolins and other related instruments, many of which appear on this recording. The concept for this project is what happens when a vintage instrument collector, a mandolin player, a record producer, and the owner of an independent acoustic label all happen to be the same person.

TURN OF THE CENTURY

By David Grisman
Transcribed by John Carlini

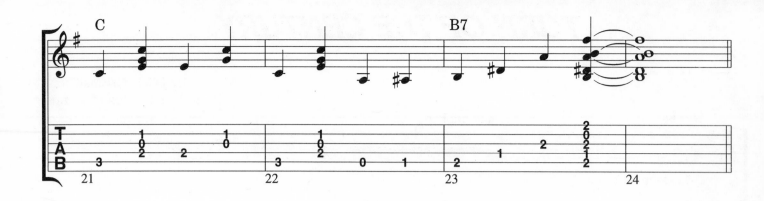

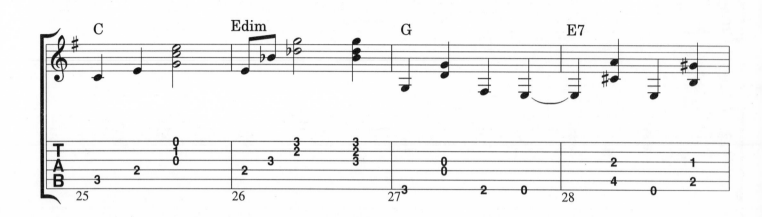

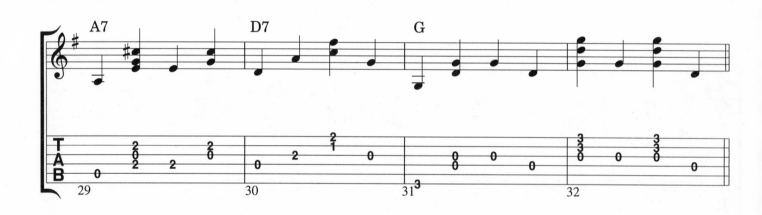

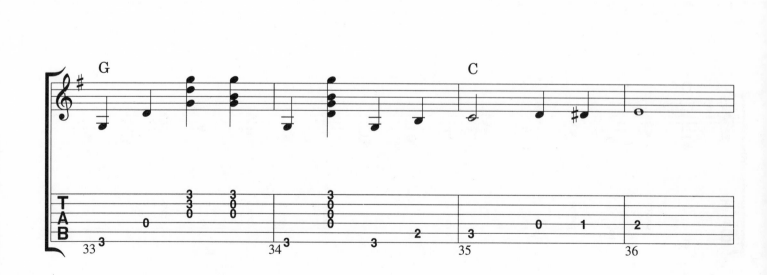

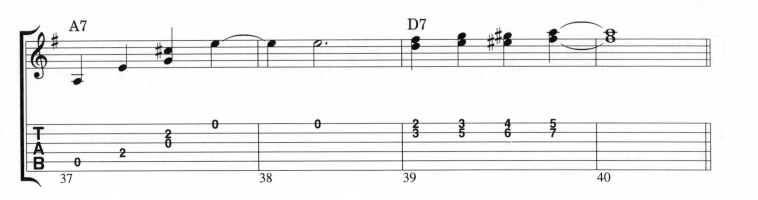

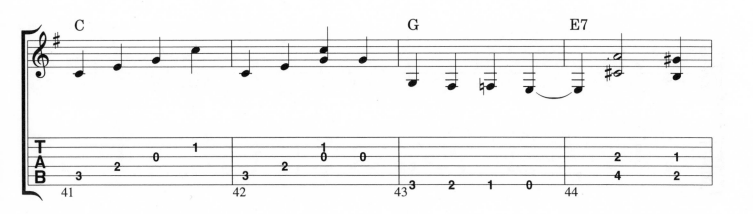

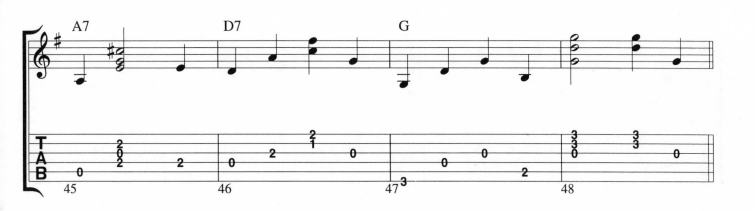

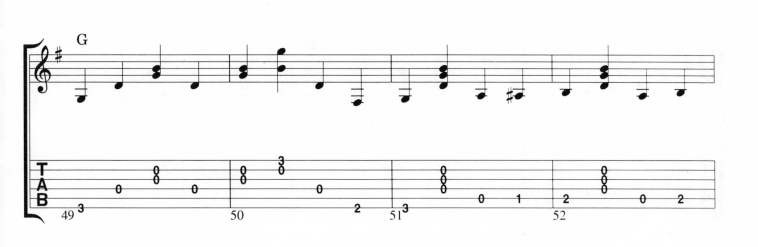

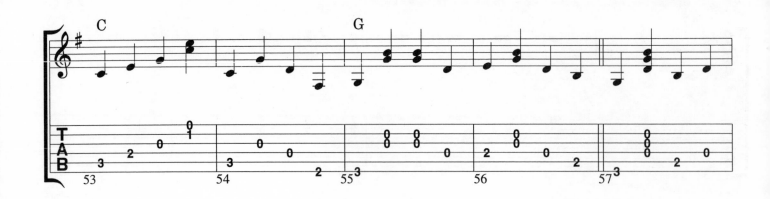

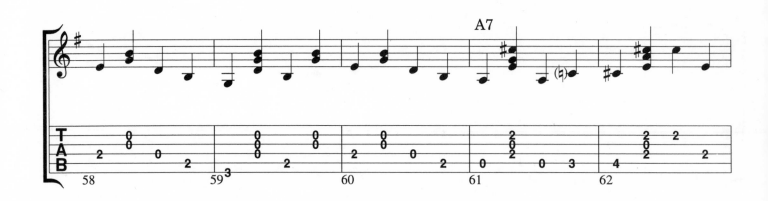

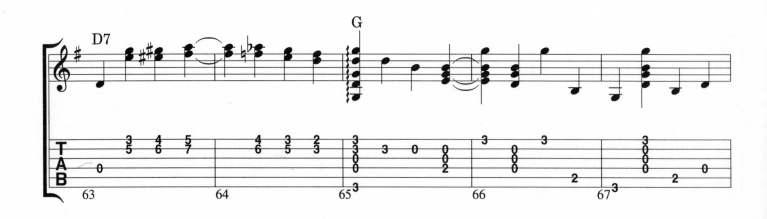

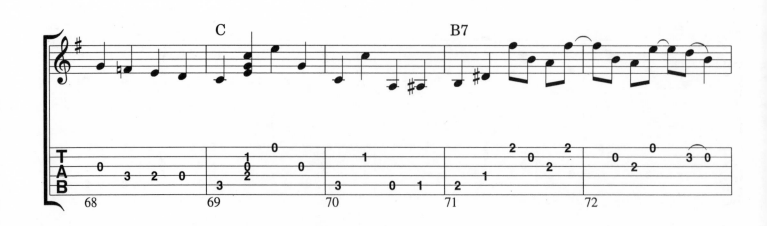

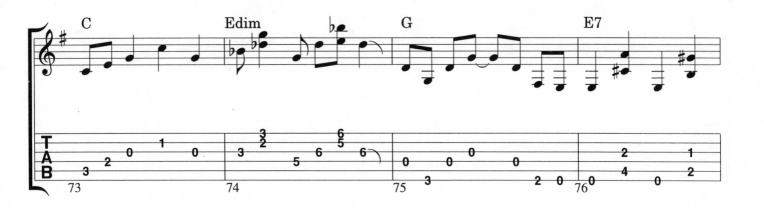

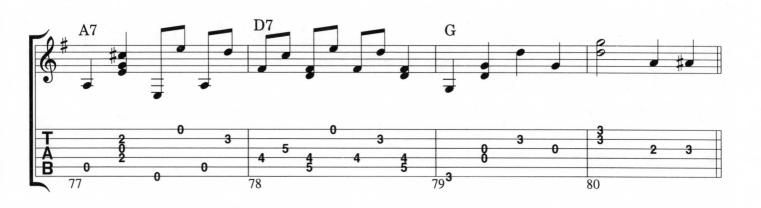

[Melodic solo in the style of Tony Rice]

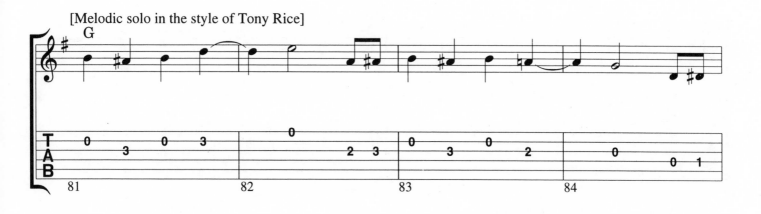

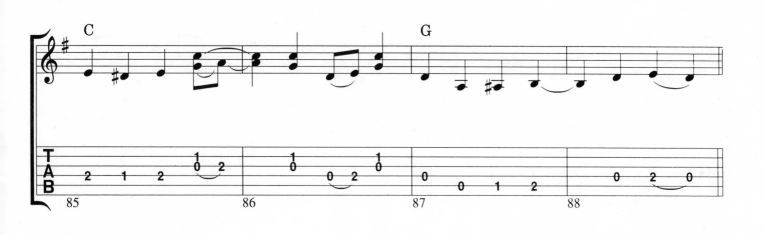

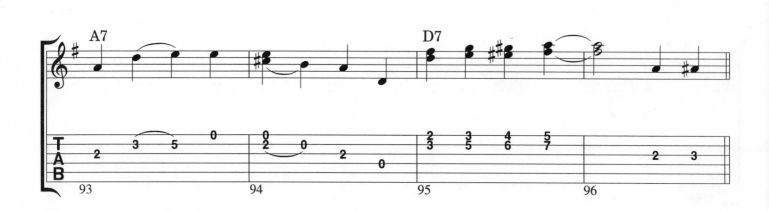

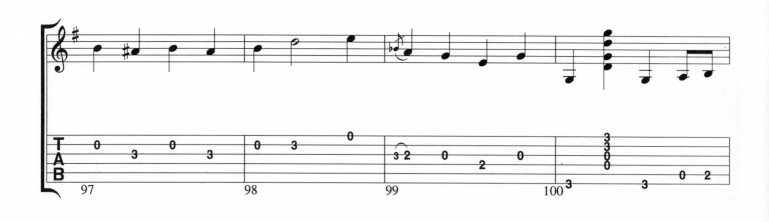

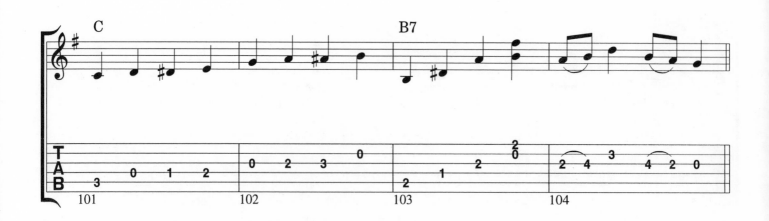

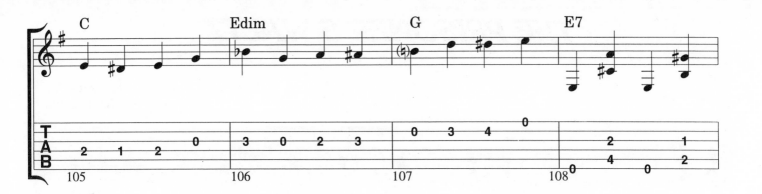

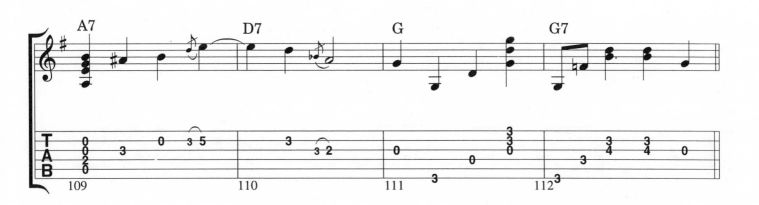

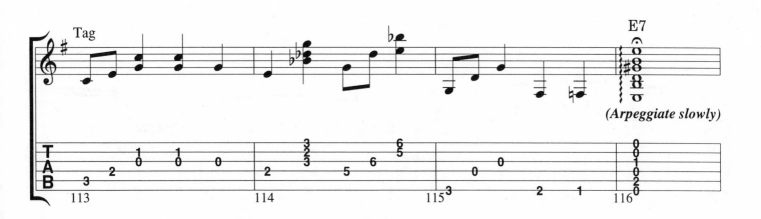

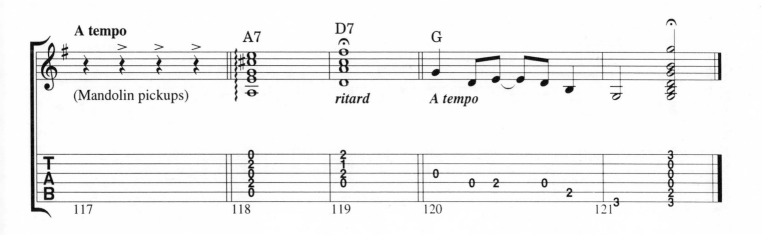

THE PRISONER'S WALTZ

By David Grisman
Transcribed by John Carlini

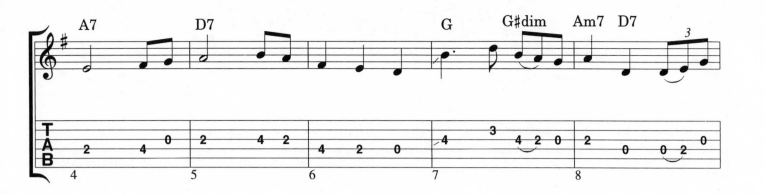

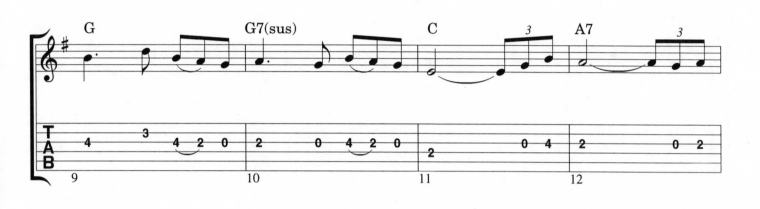

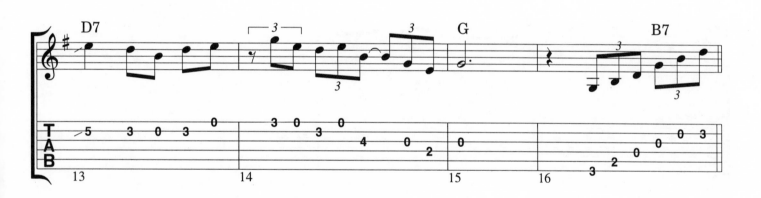

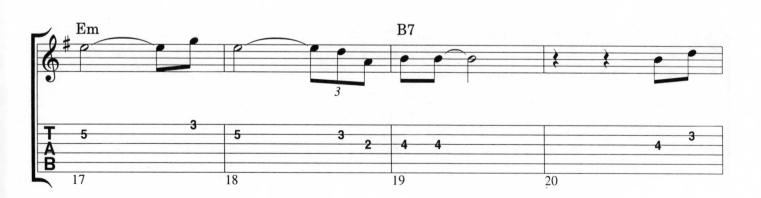

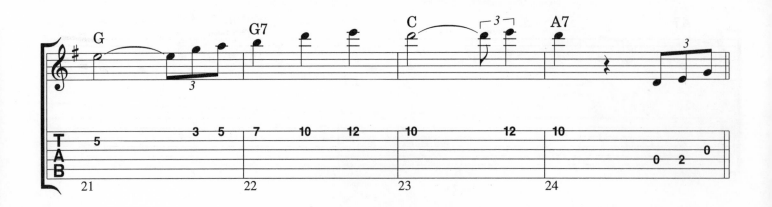
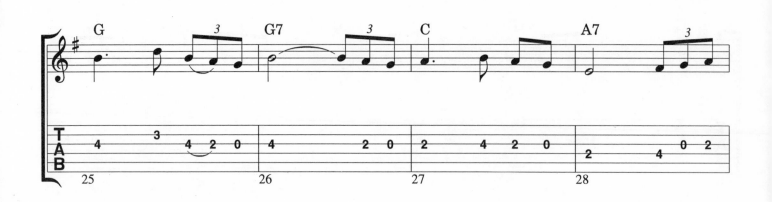
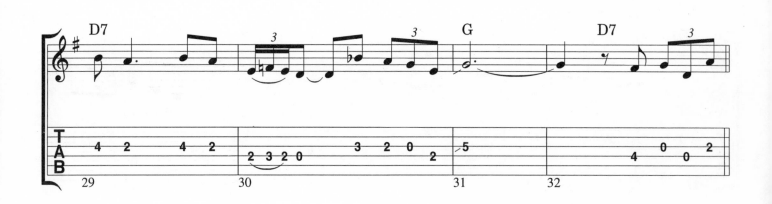
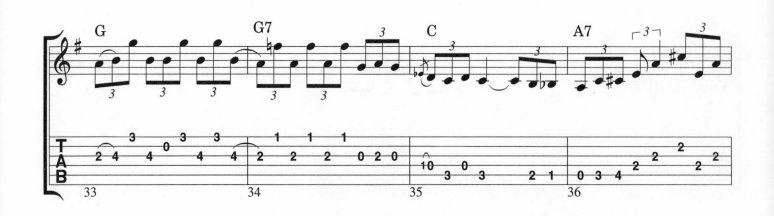

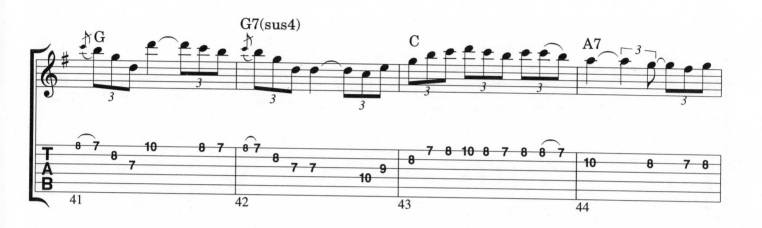

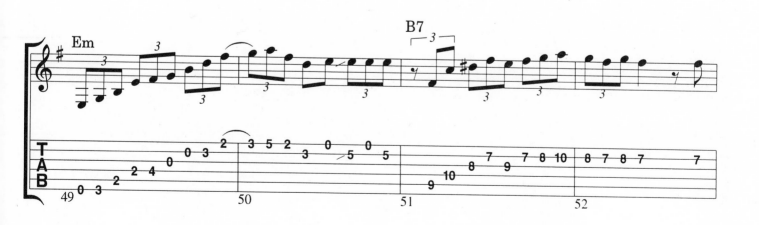

15

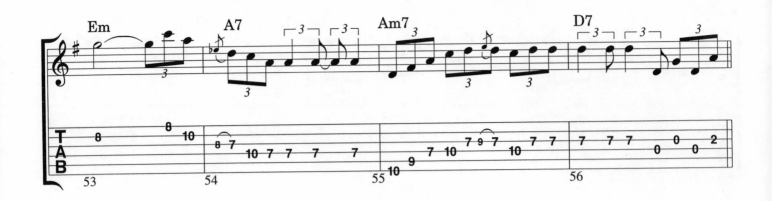

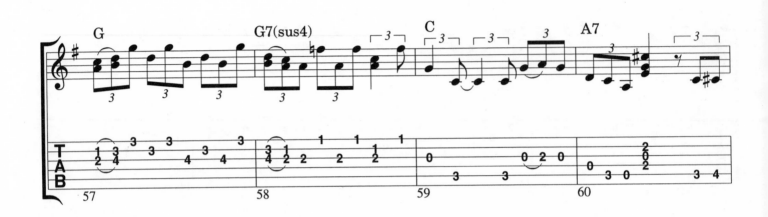

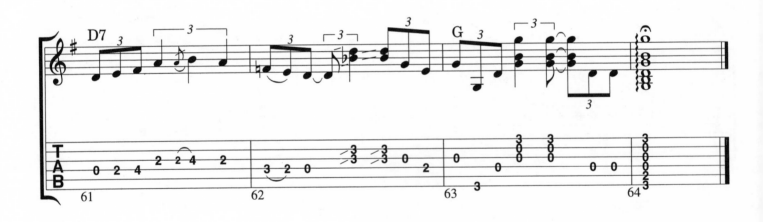

SAM-BINO

By David Grisman
Transcribed by John Carlini

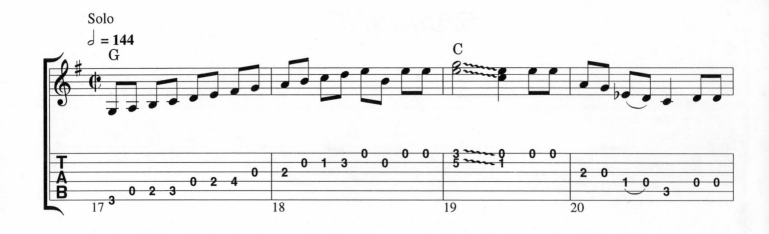

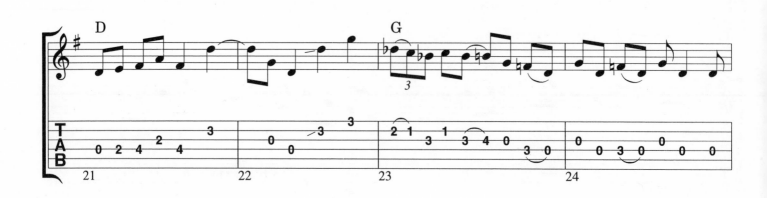

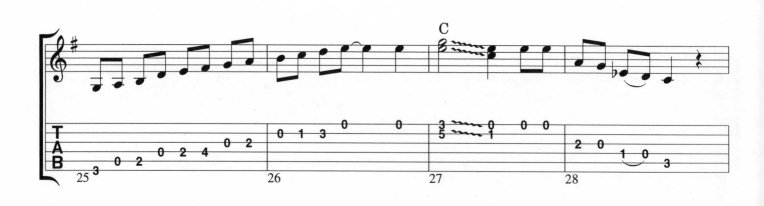

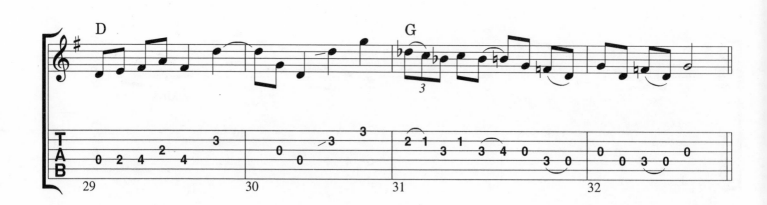

GRANDFATHER'S CLOCK

Trad. Arr. David Grisman
Transcribed by John Carlini

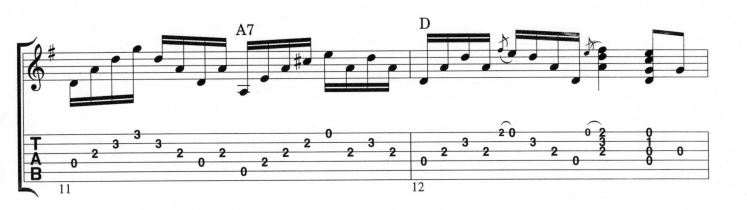

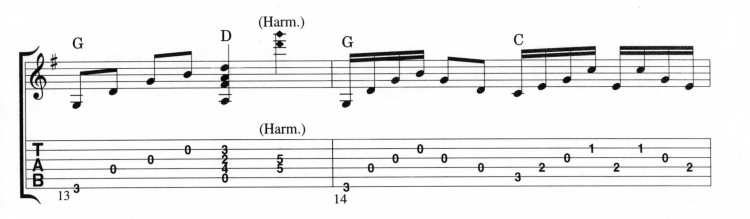

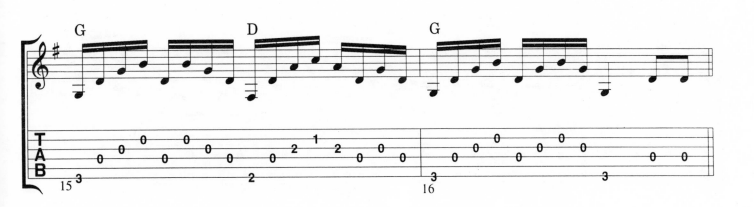

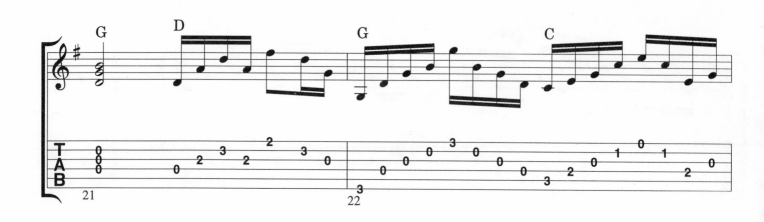

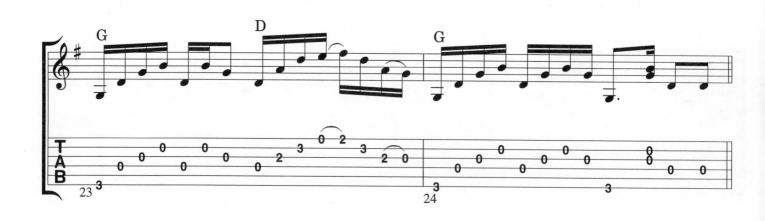

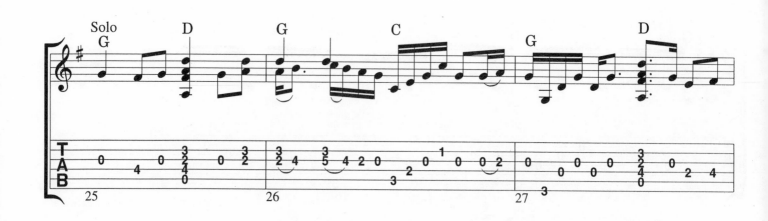

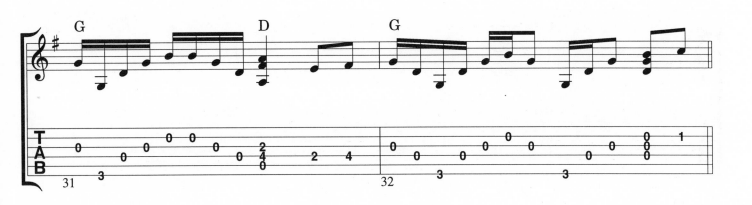

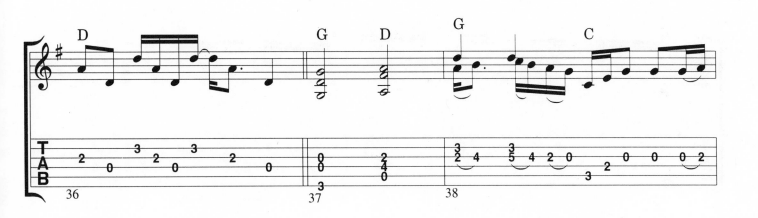

23

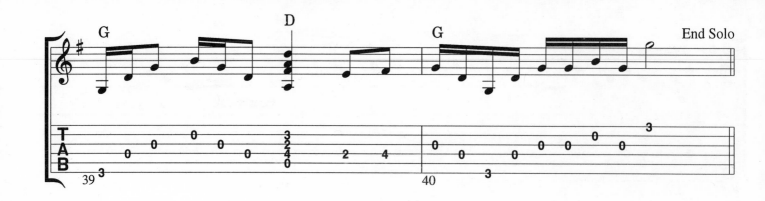

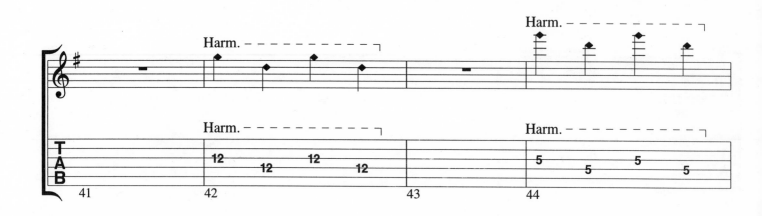

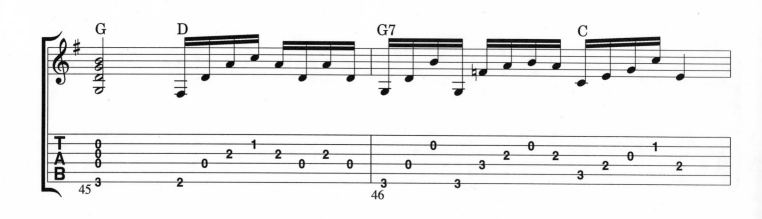

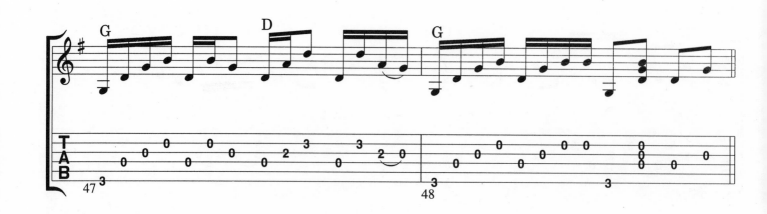

24

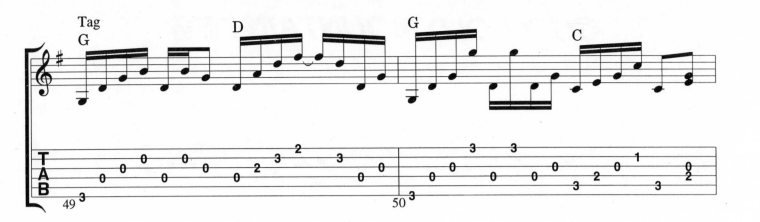

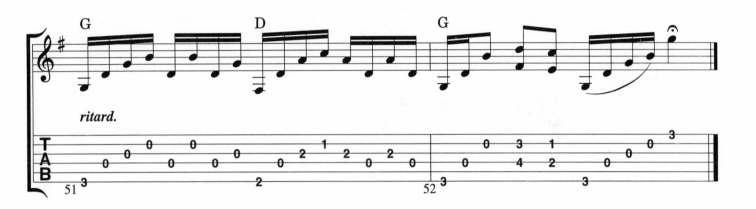

25

GOOD OLD MOUNTAIN DEW

Capo at 2nd fret

Trad. Arr. David Grisman
Transcribed by John Carlini

26

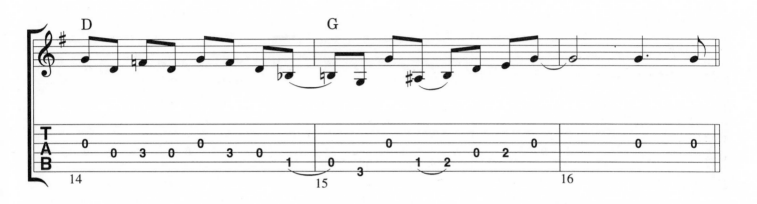

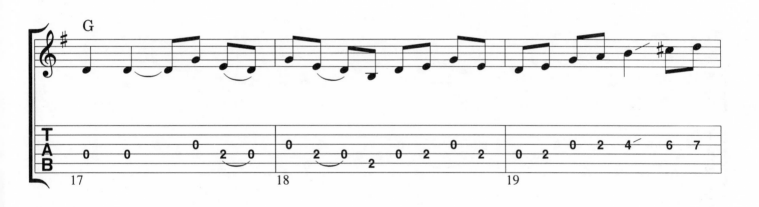

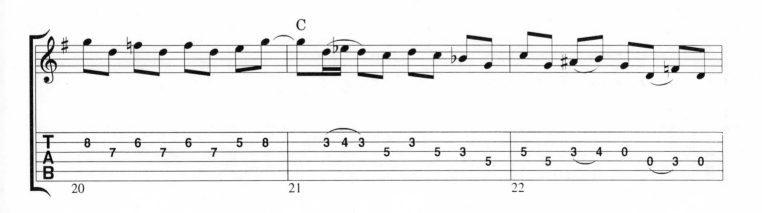

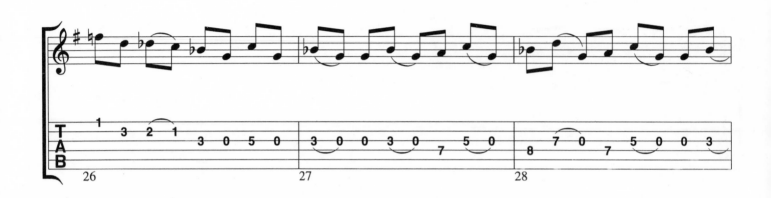
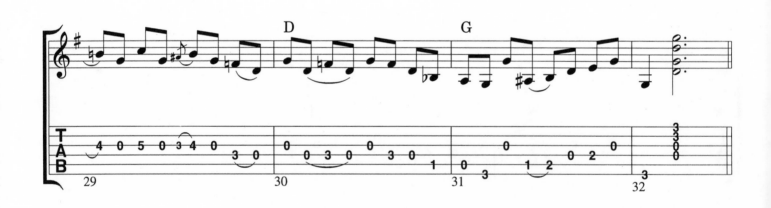
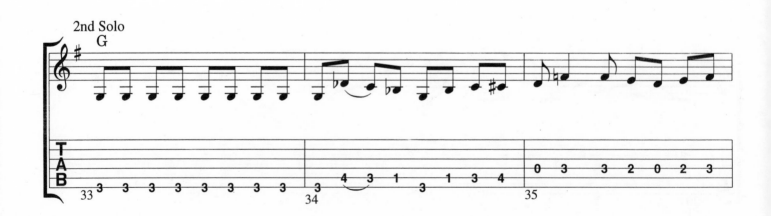

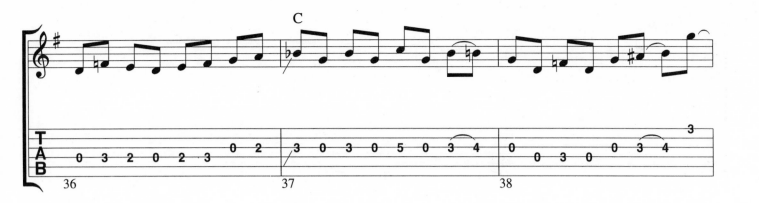

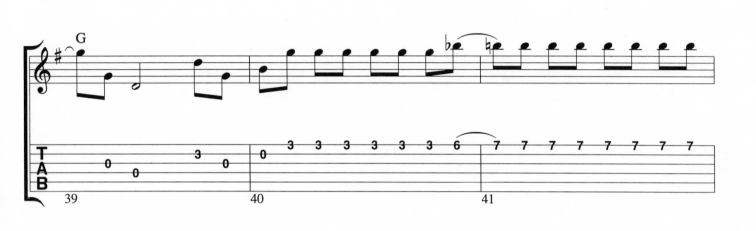

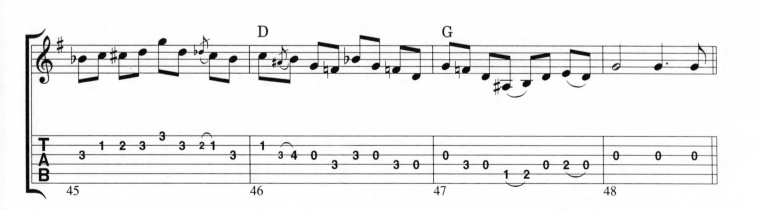

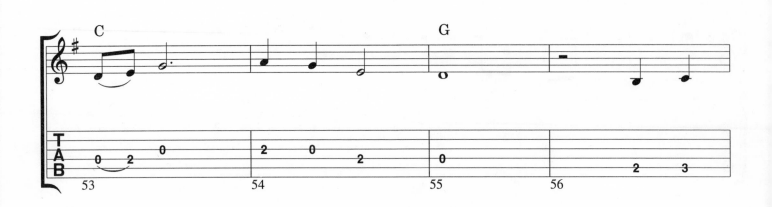

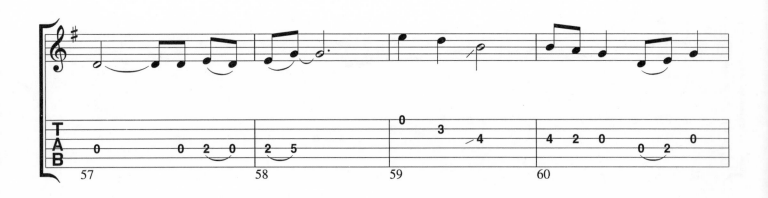

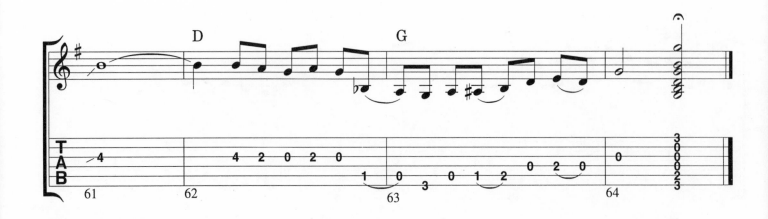

I AM A PILGRIM

Trad. By David Grisman
Transcribed by John Carlini

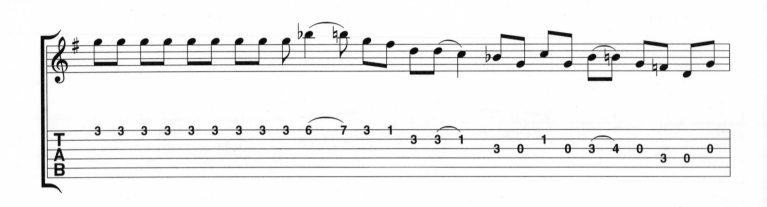

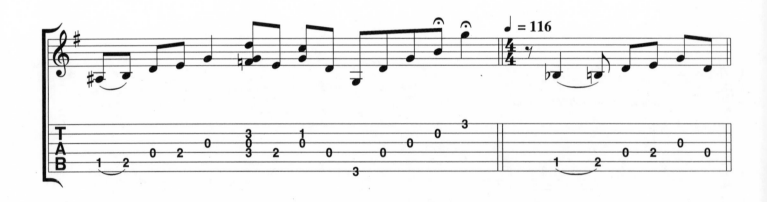

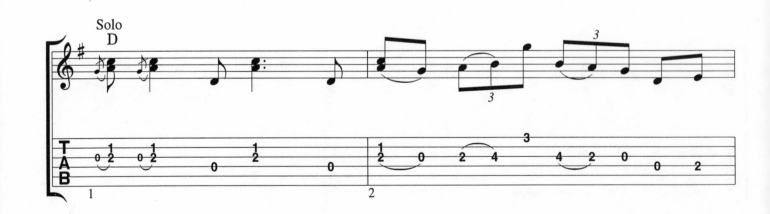

32

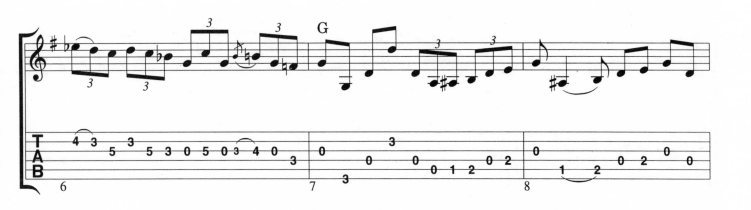

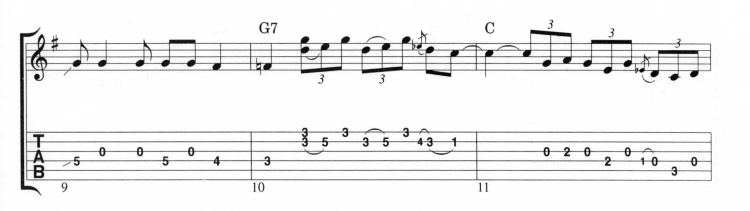

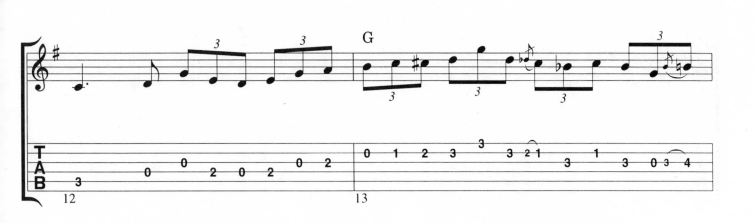

2nd Chorus

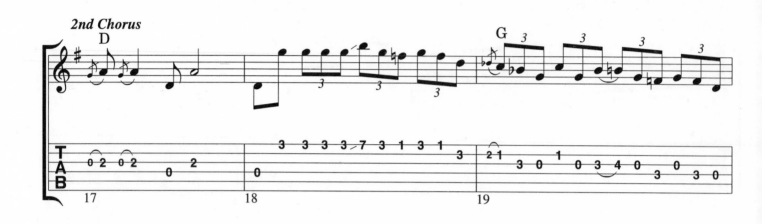

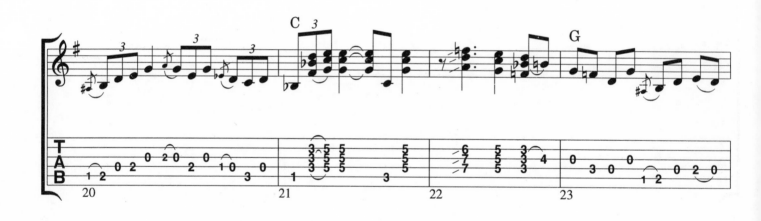

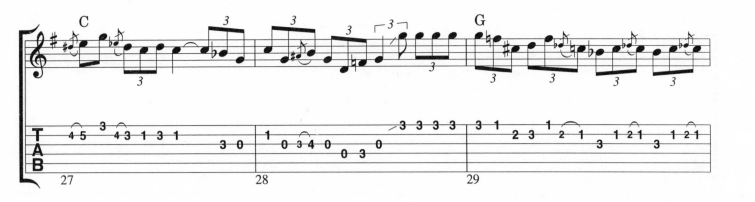

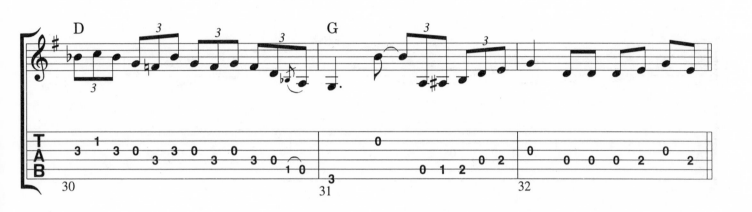

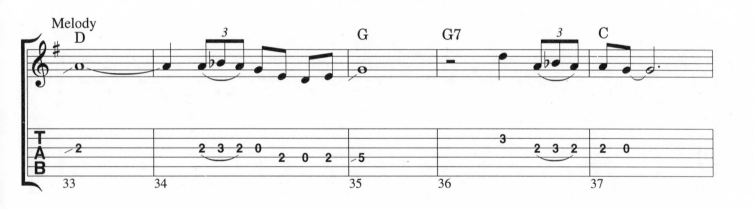

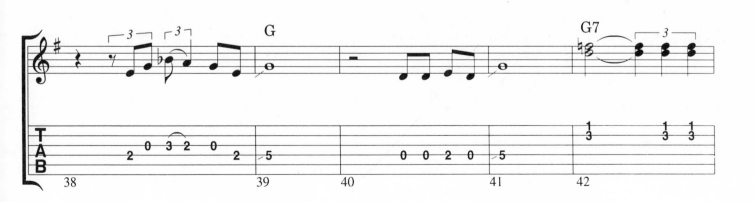

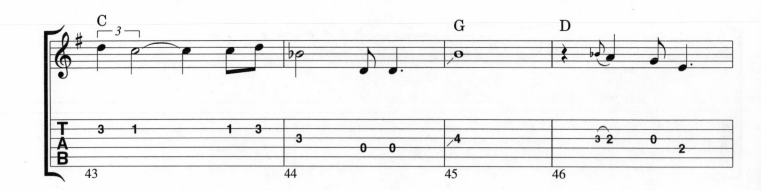

MILL VALLEY WALTZ

By David Grisman
Transcribed by John Carlini

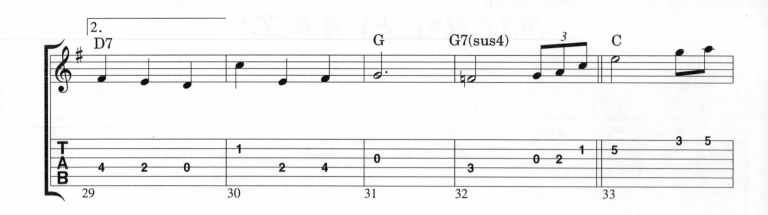
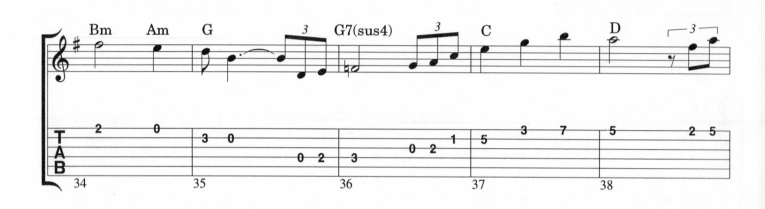
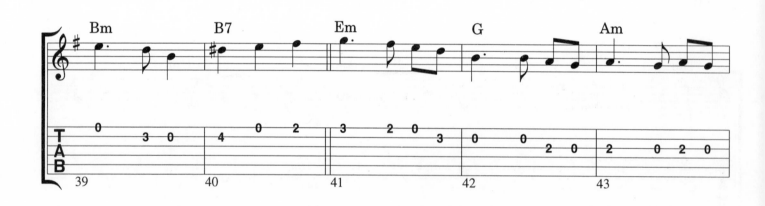
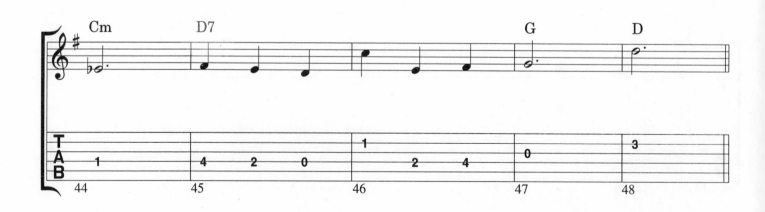

(Solo in the style of Tony Rice)

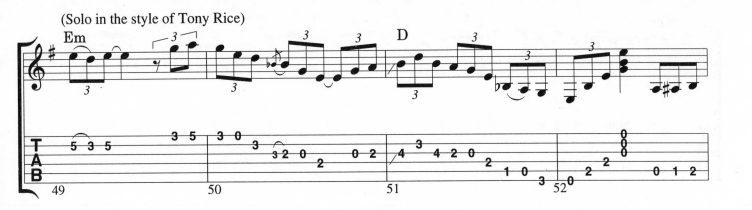

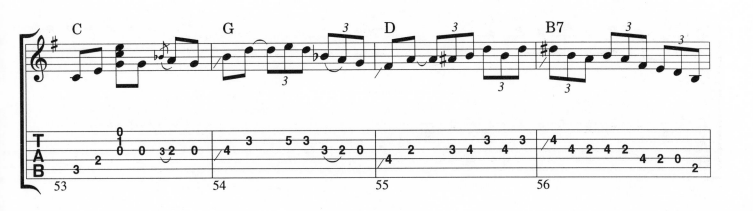

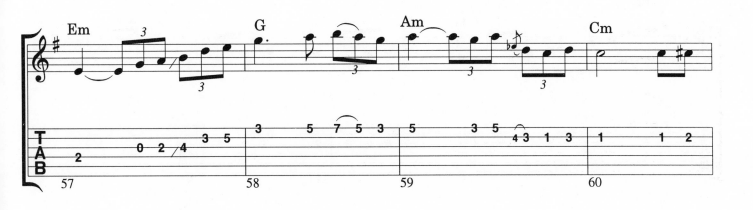

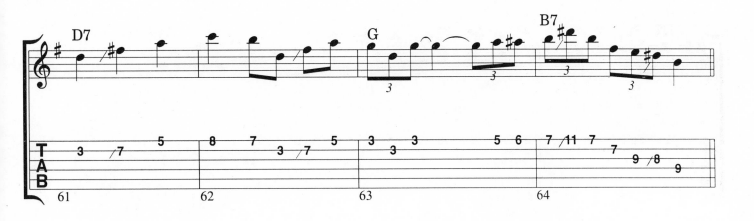

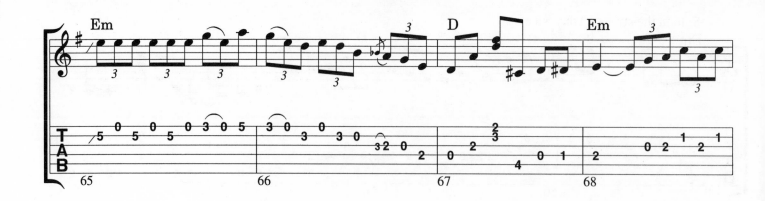
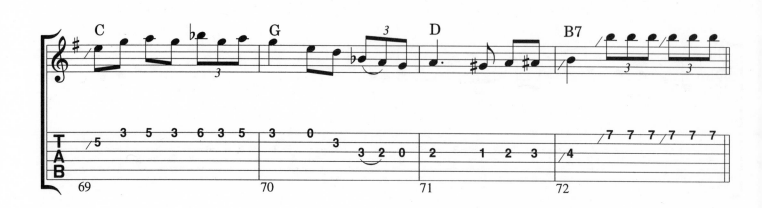
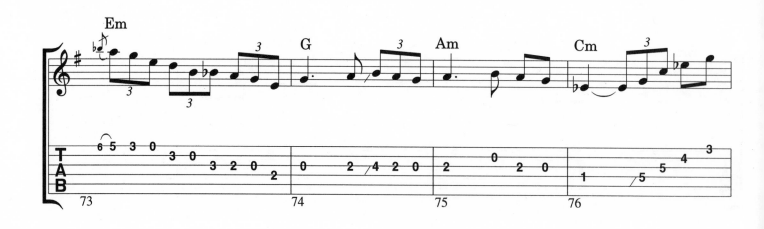
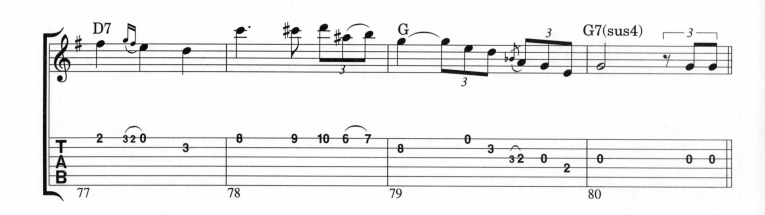

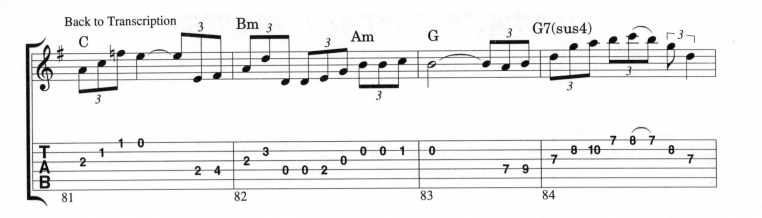
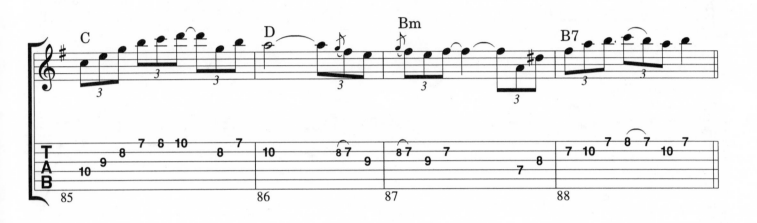
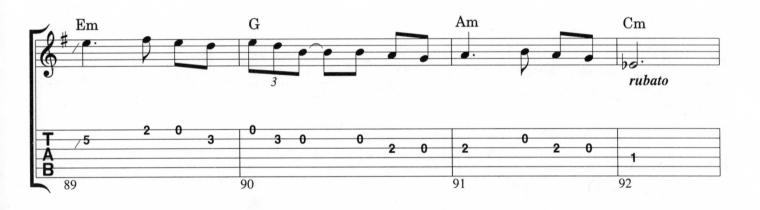
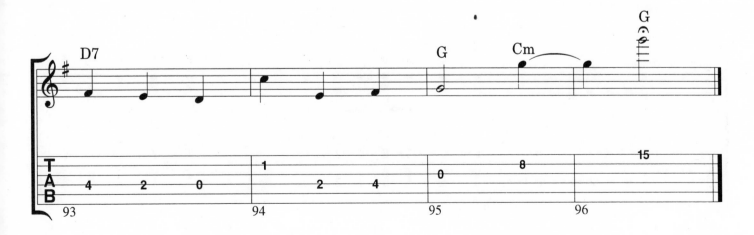

41

VINTAGE GINTAGE BLUES

By David Grisman
Transcribed by John Carlini

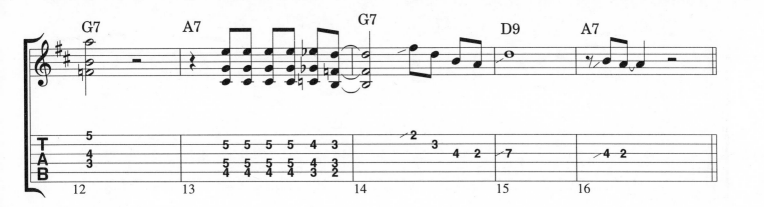

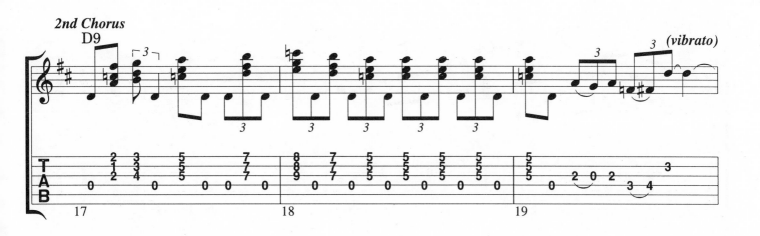

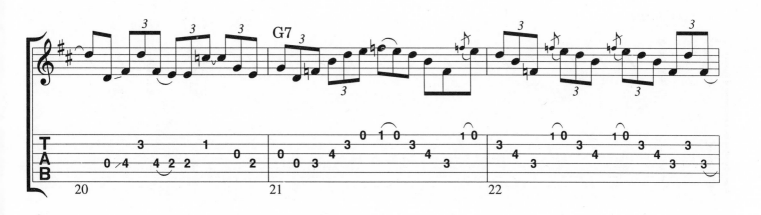

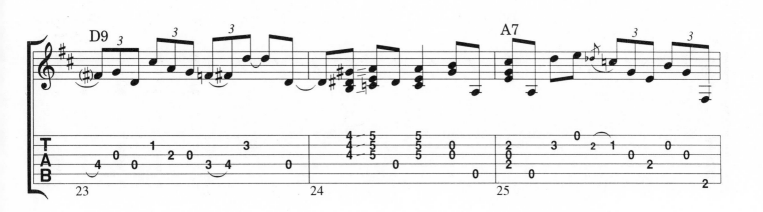

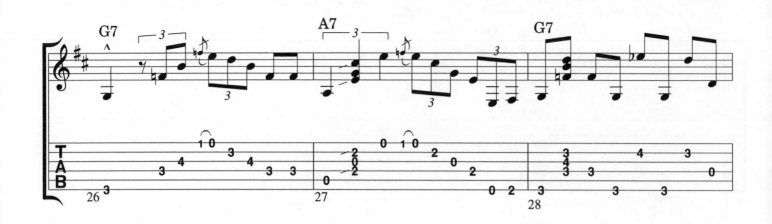

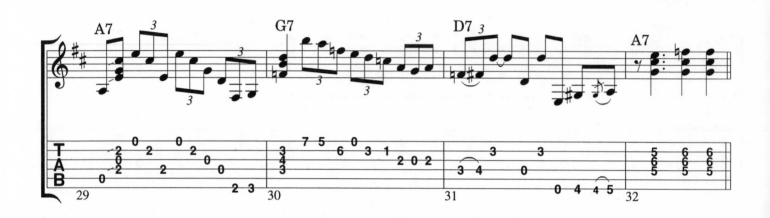

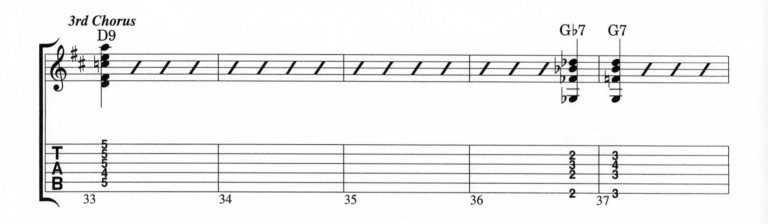

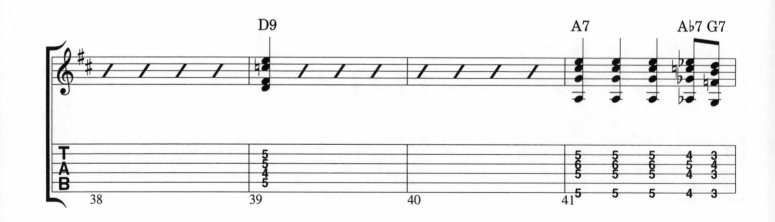

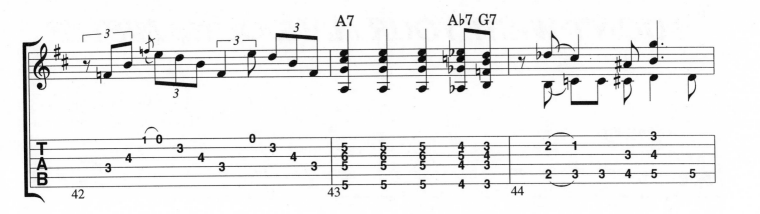

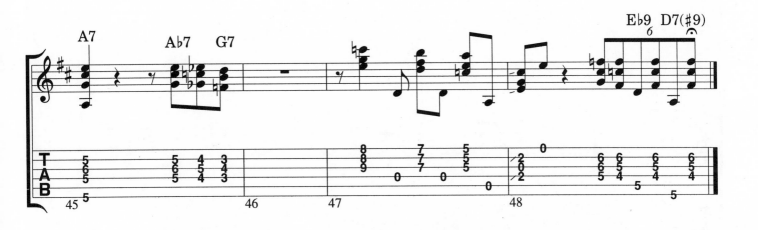

I DON'T WANT YOUR MANDOLINS MISTER

Trad. Arr. David Grisman
Transcribed by John Carlini

46

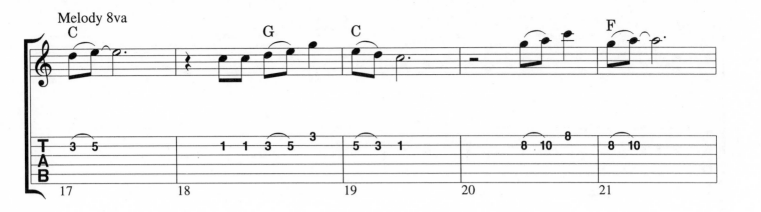

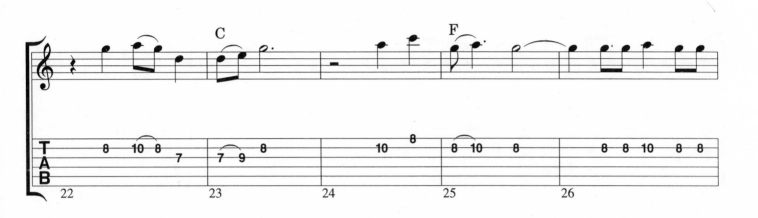

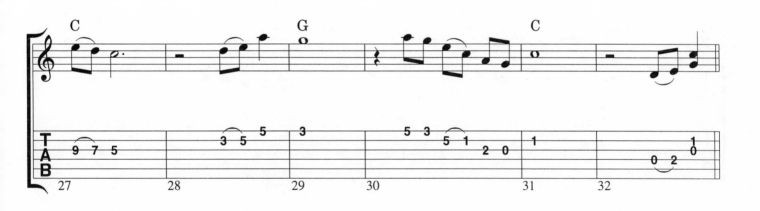

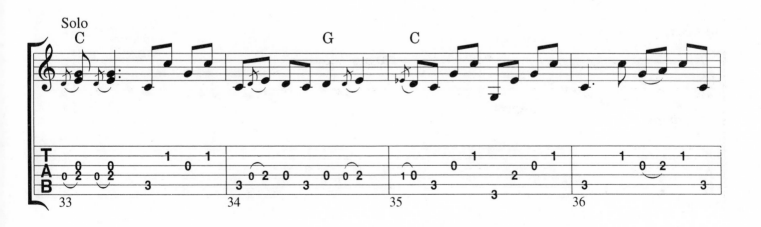

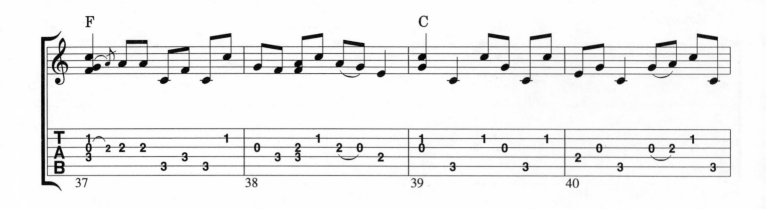

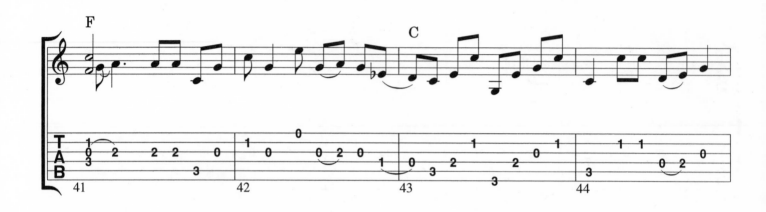

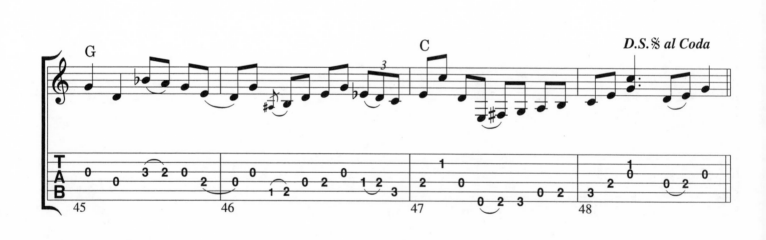

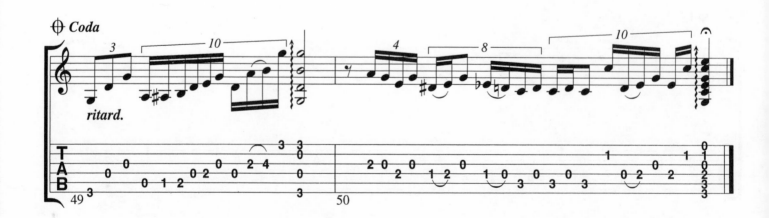

DAWG AFTER DARK

By David Grisman
Transcribed by John Carlini

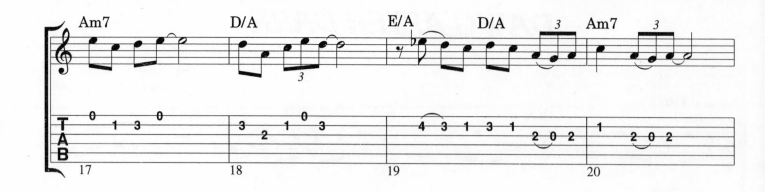

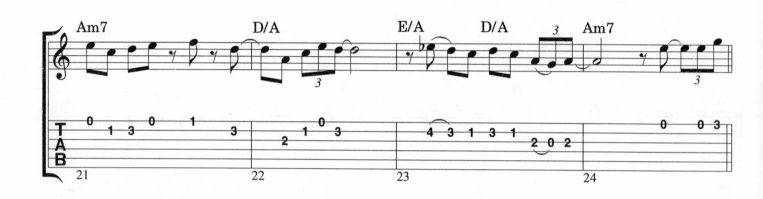

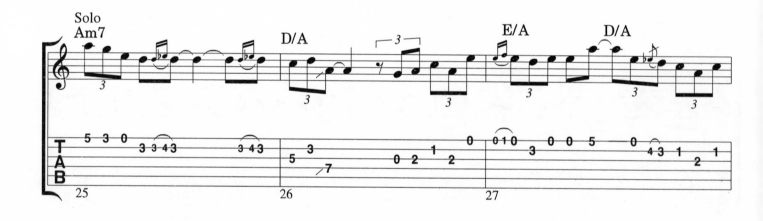

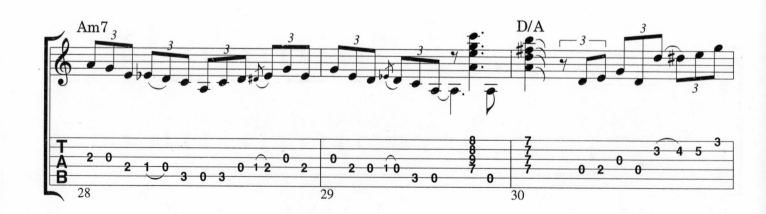

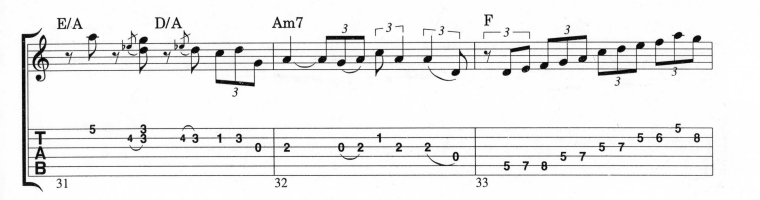

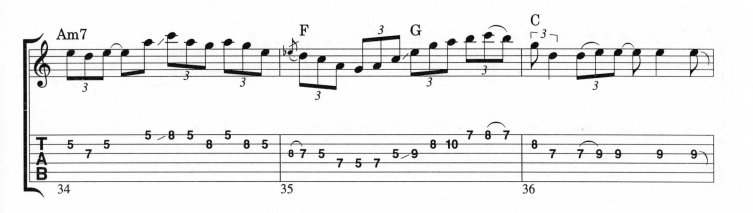

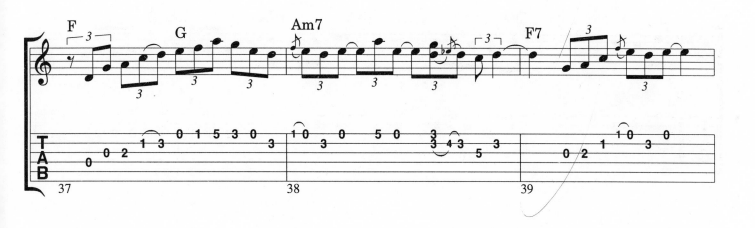

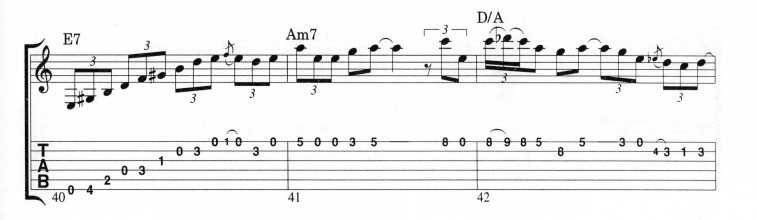

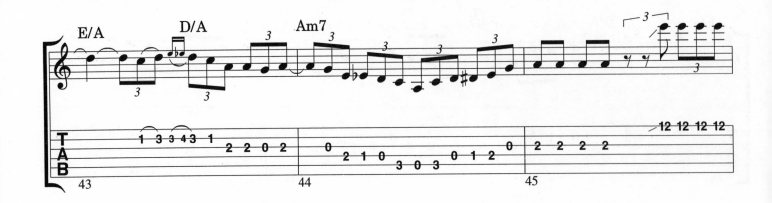

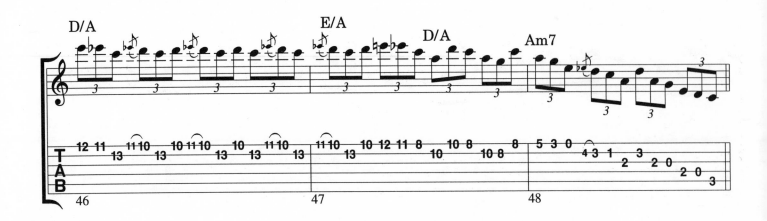

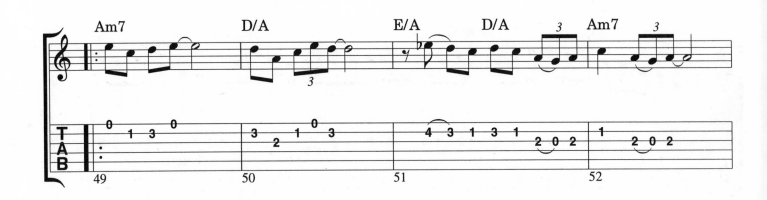

Repeat last 8 bars as many times as needed.

WILDWOOD FLOWER

C / Capo 4th fret

Trad. Arr. David Grisman
Transcribed by John Carlini

53

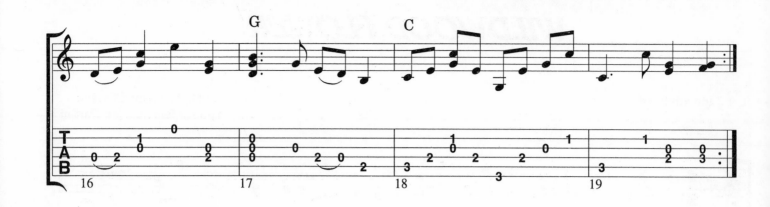

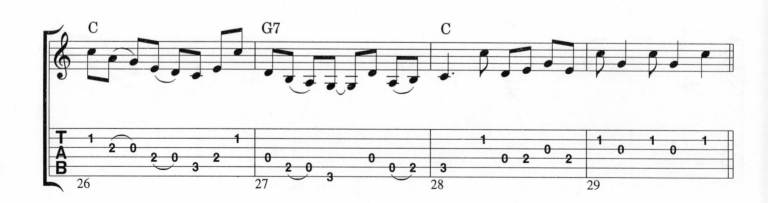

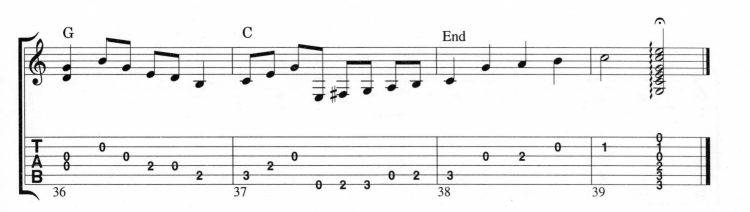

MORNING SUN

By David Grisman
Transcribed by John Carlini

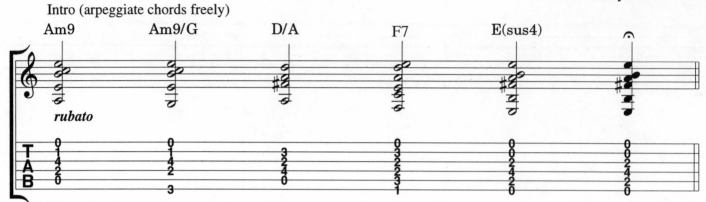

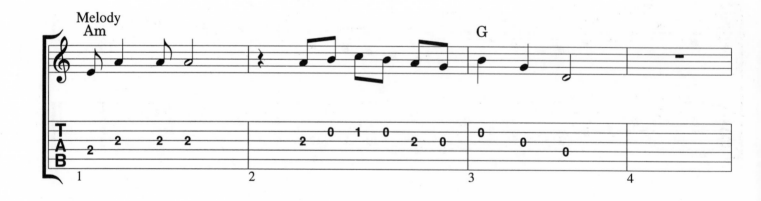

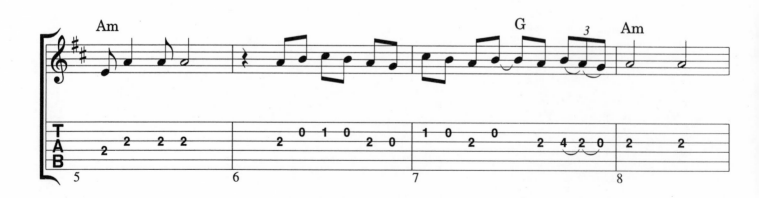

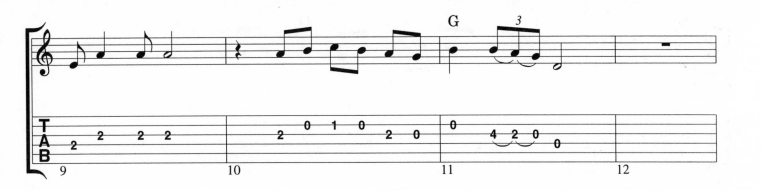
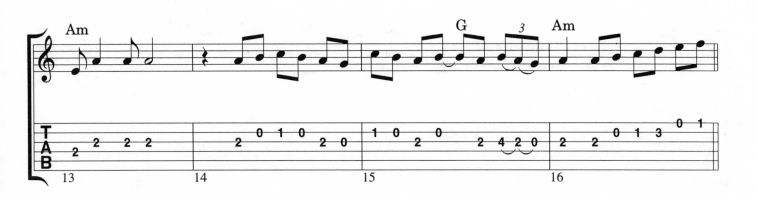
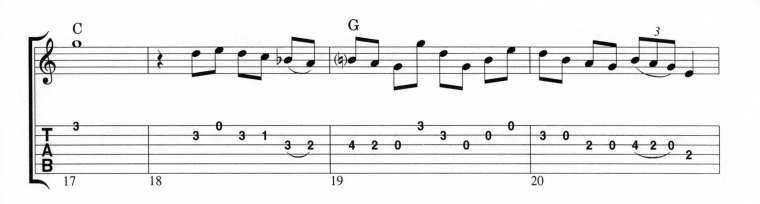
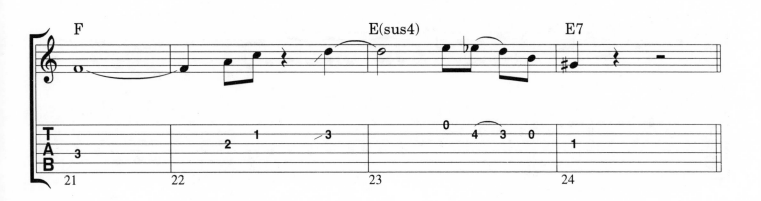

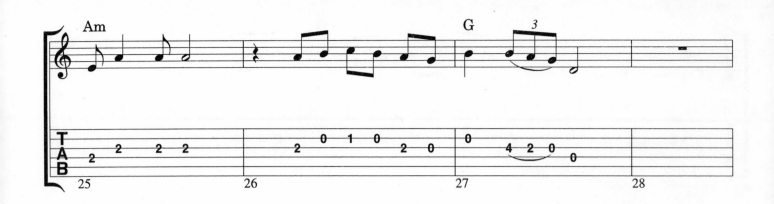

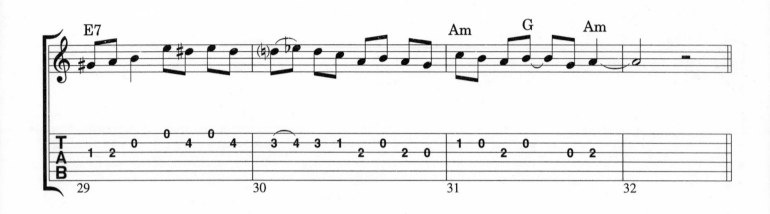

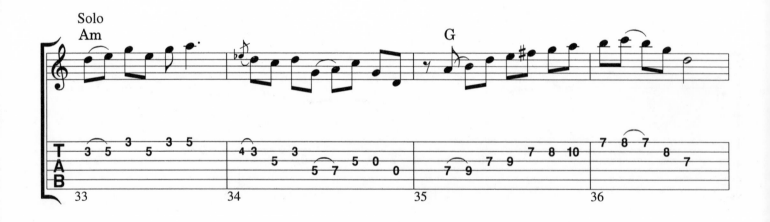

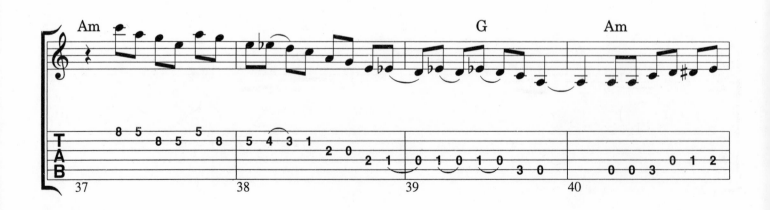

58

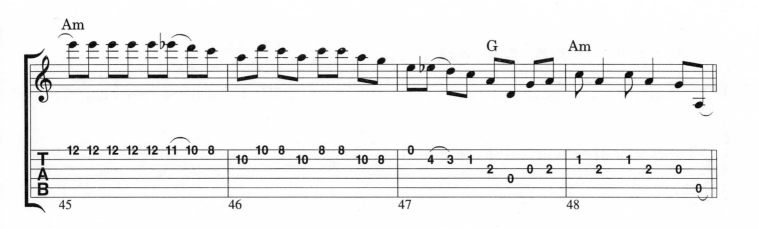
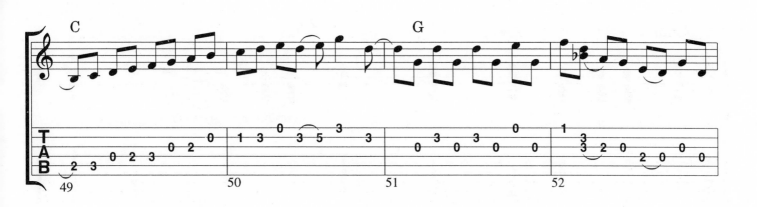
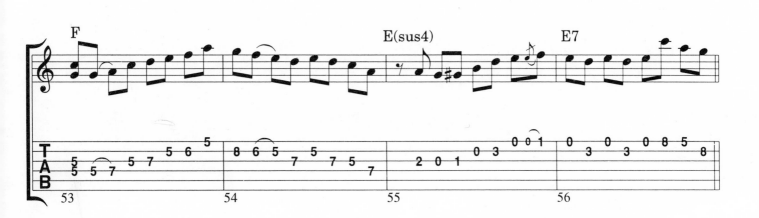

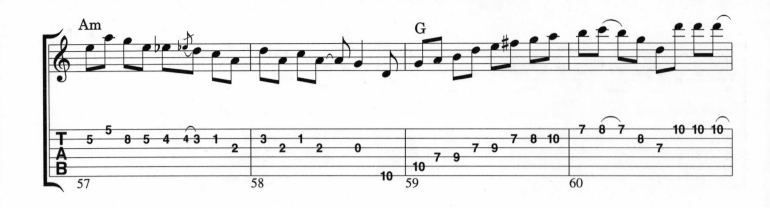

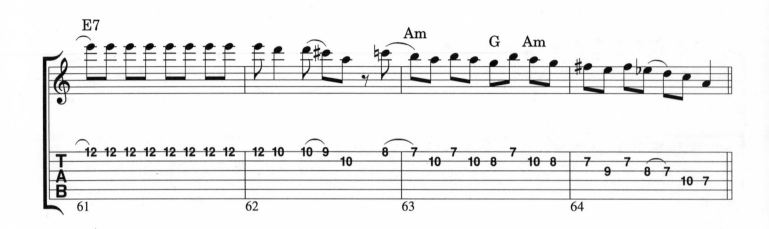

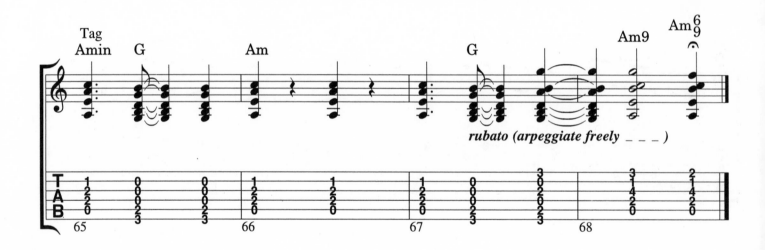

*This page has been
left blank to avoid
awkward page turns*

BANKS OF THE OHIO

Capo 2nd fret

Trad. Arr. David Grisman
Transcribed by John Carlini

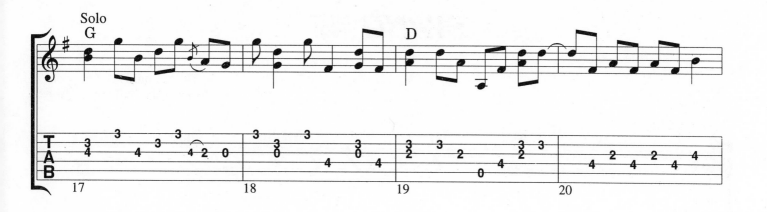

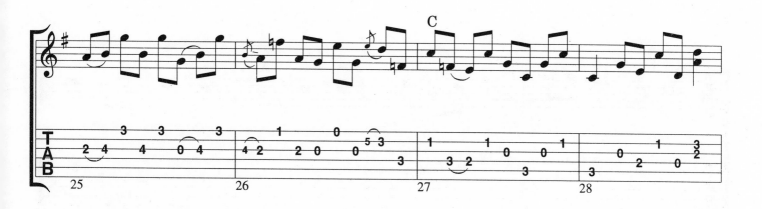

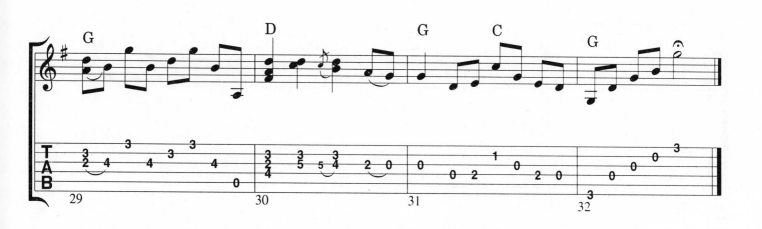

SWING '42

By D. Reinhardt/ S. Grappelli
Transcribed by John Carlini

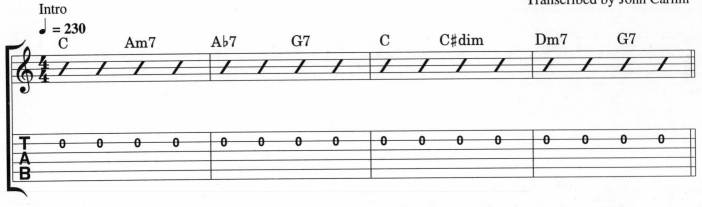

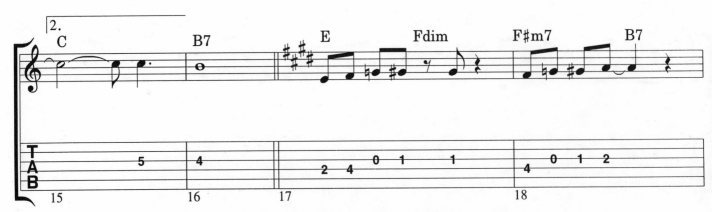

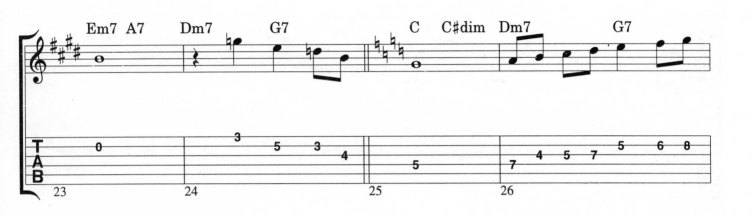

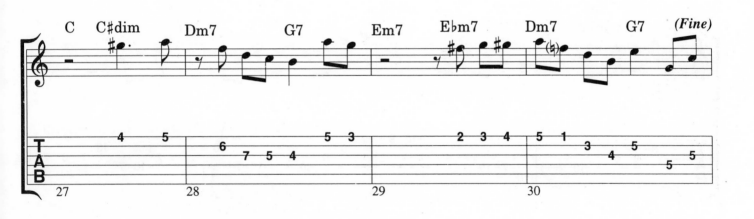

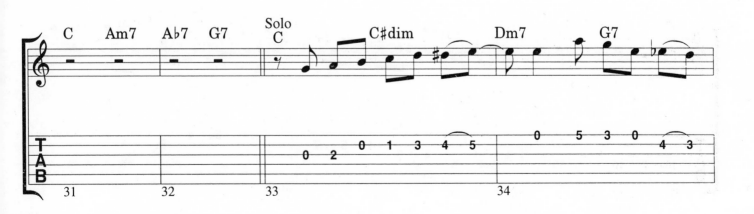

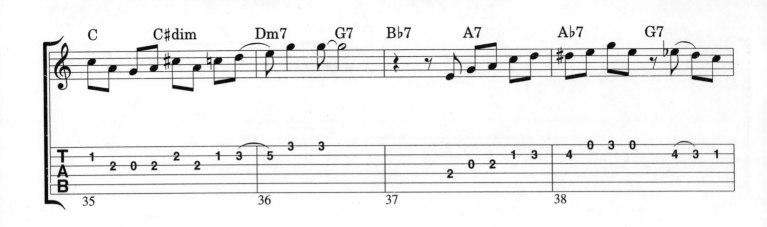

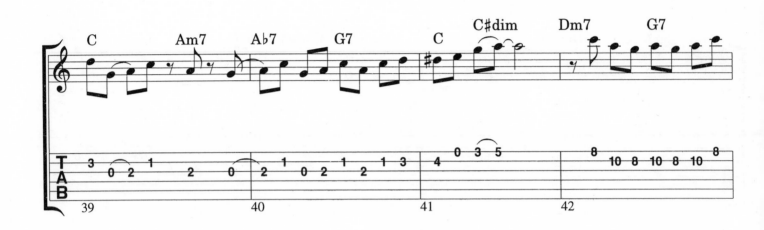

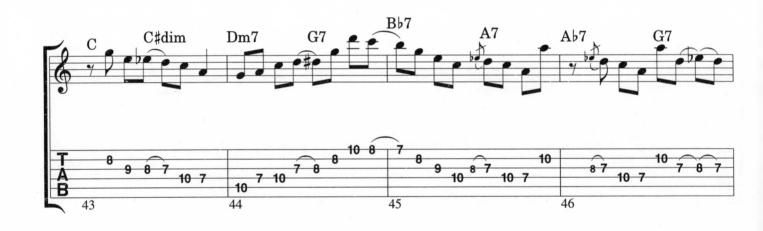

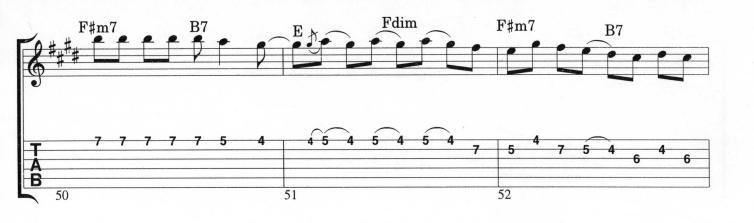

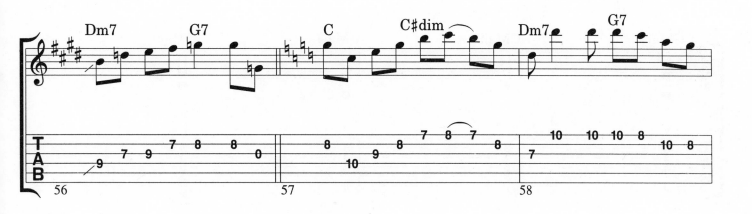

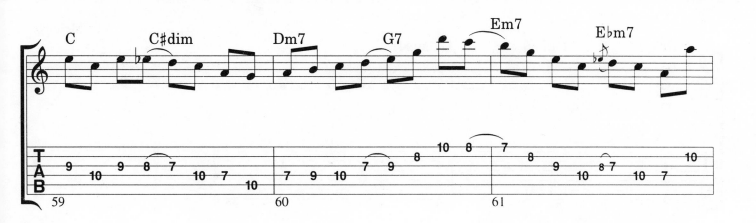

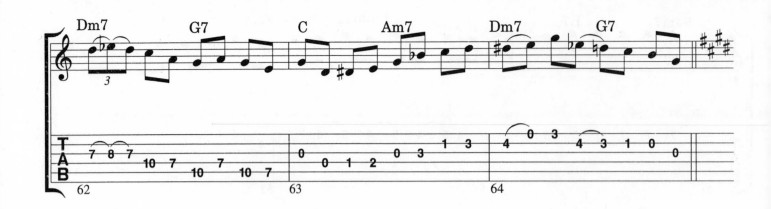

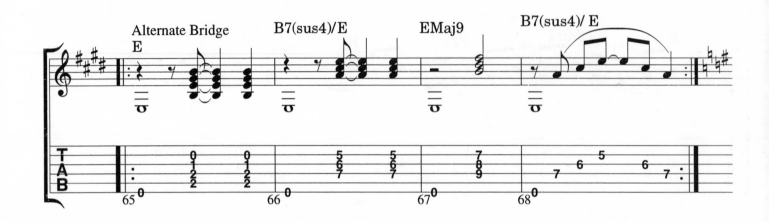

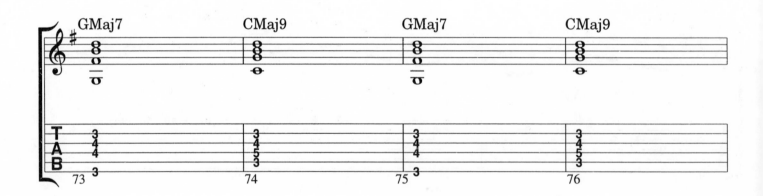

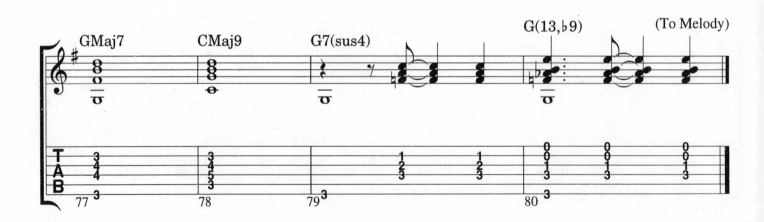

WATSON BLUES

By Bill Monroe
Transcribed by John Carlini

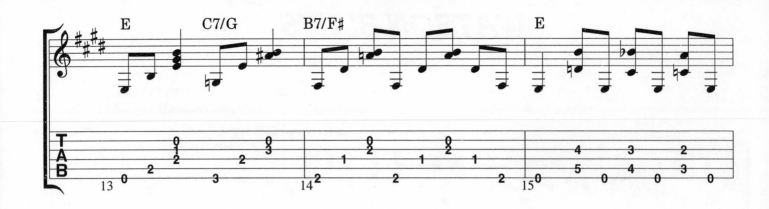

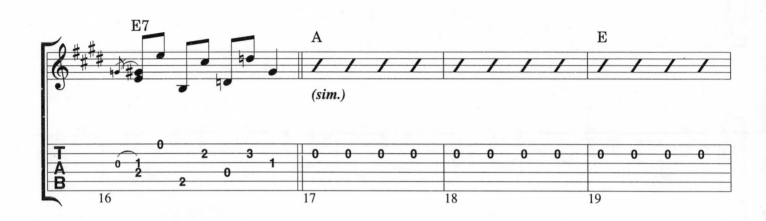

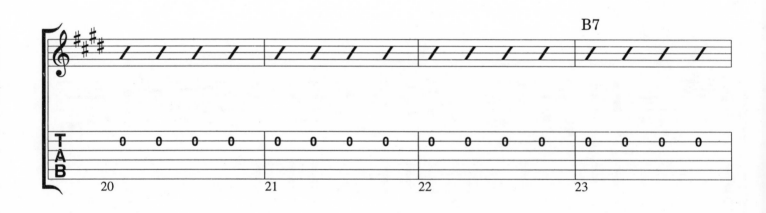

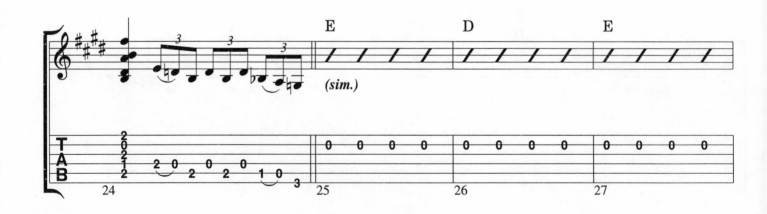

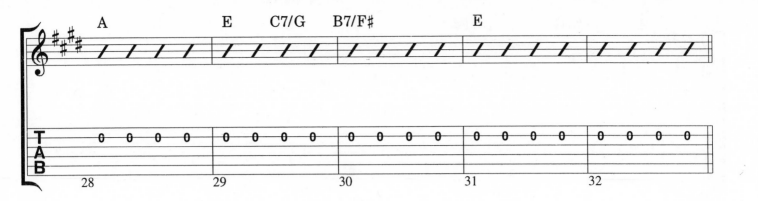

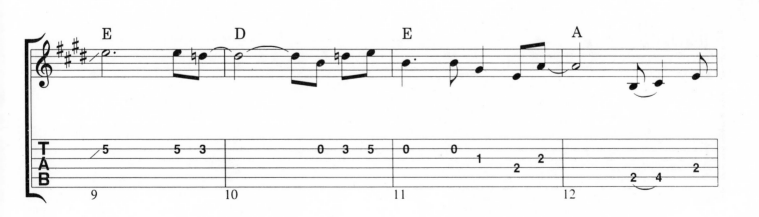

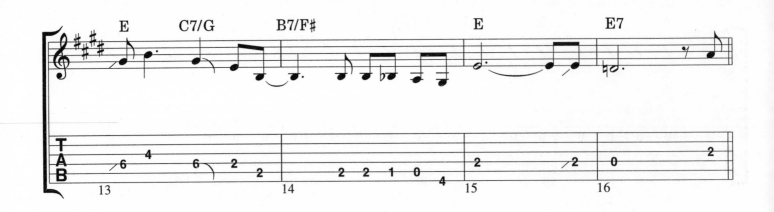

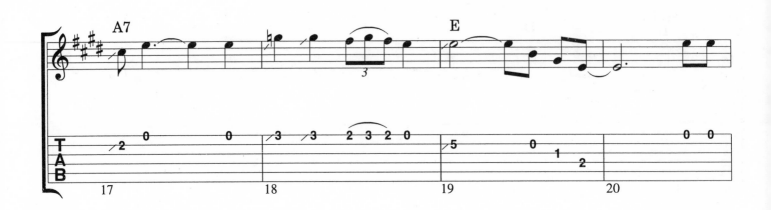

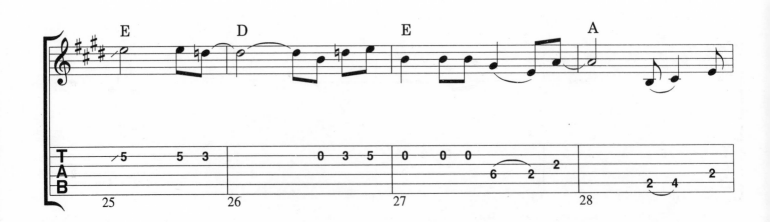

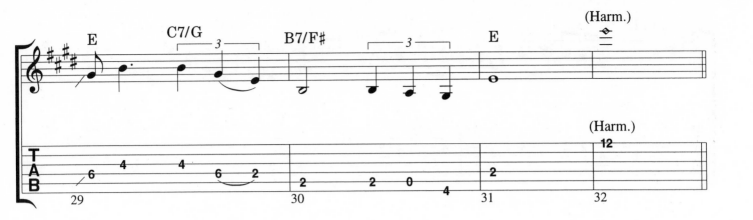

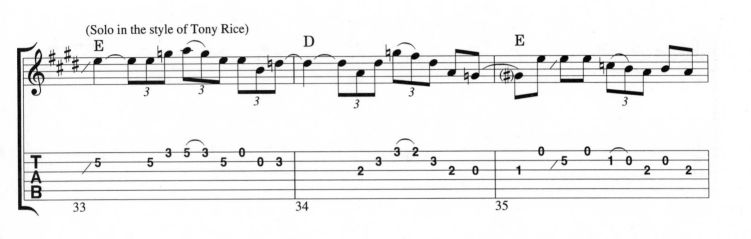

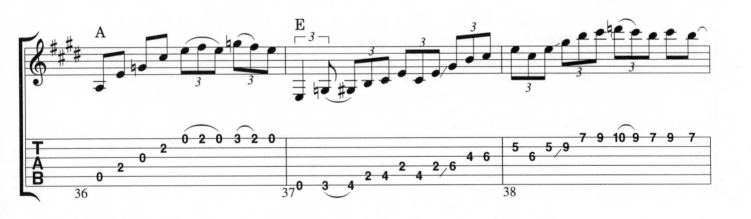

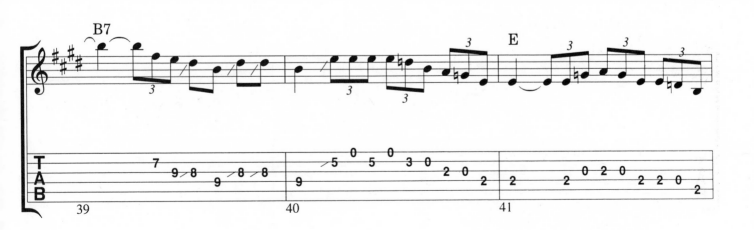

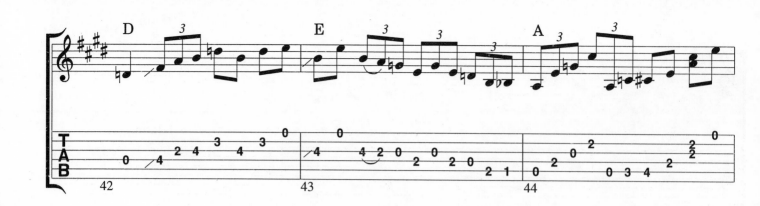

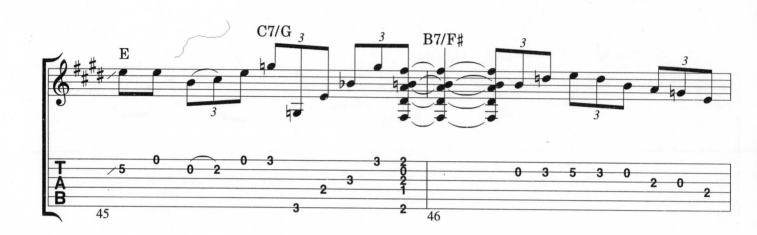

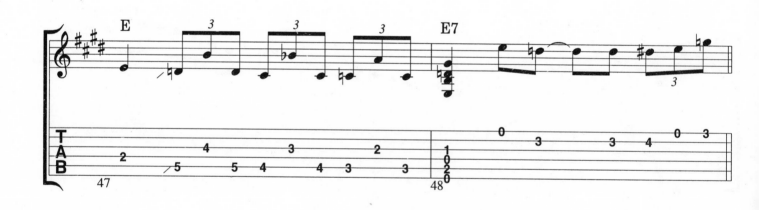

Back to Transcription

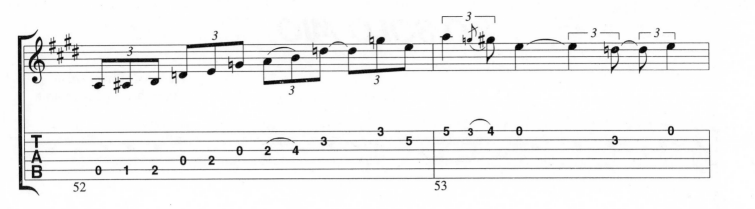

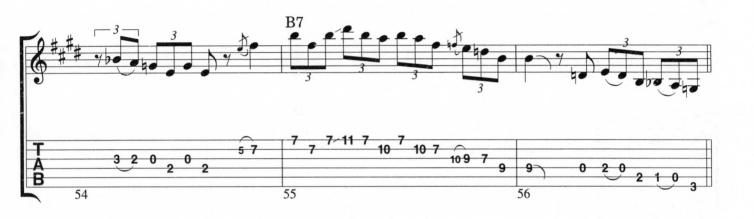

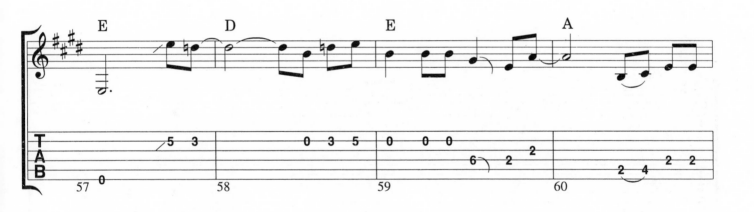

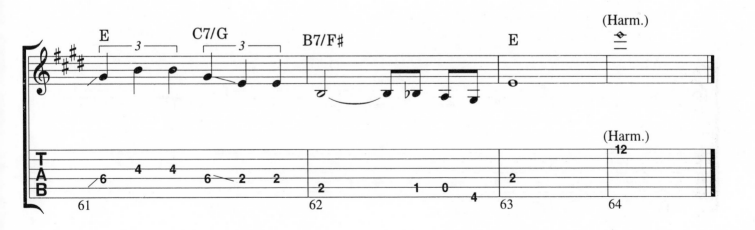

O SOLO MIO

Trad. Arr. David Grisman
Transcribed by John Carlini

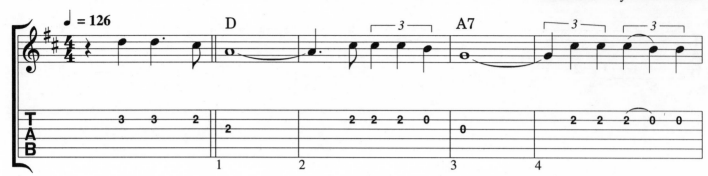

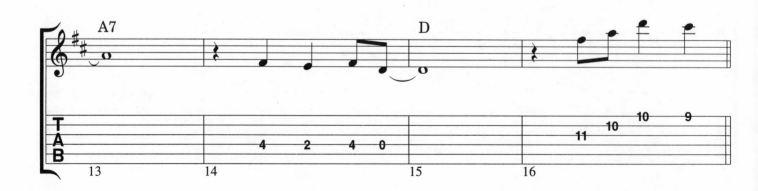

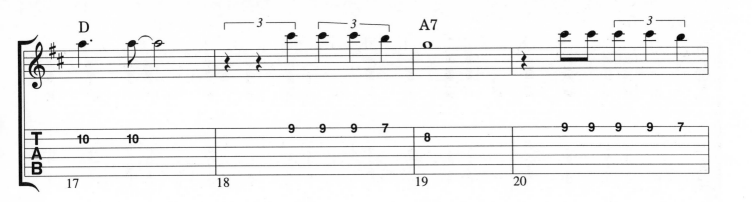

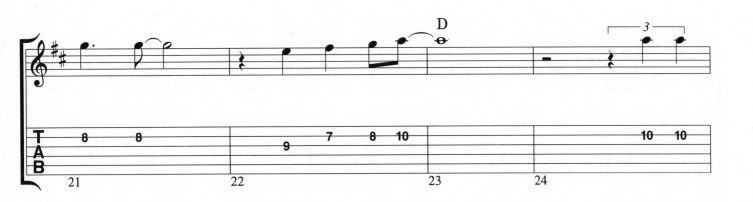

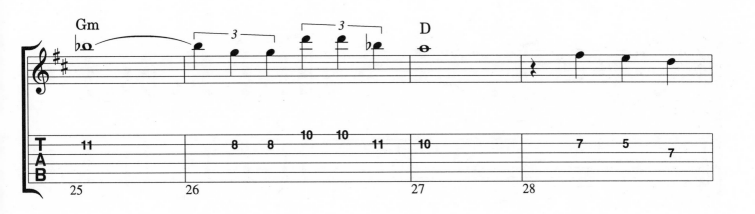

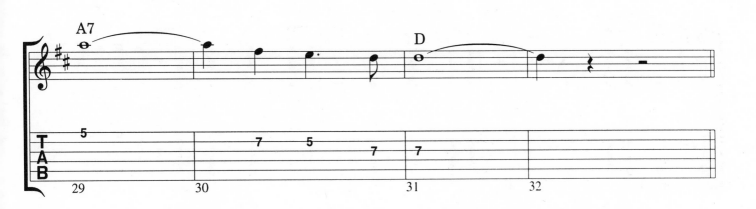

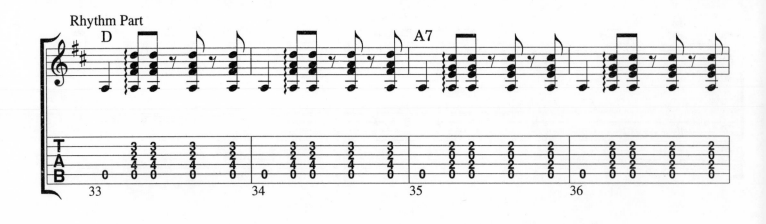

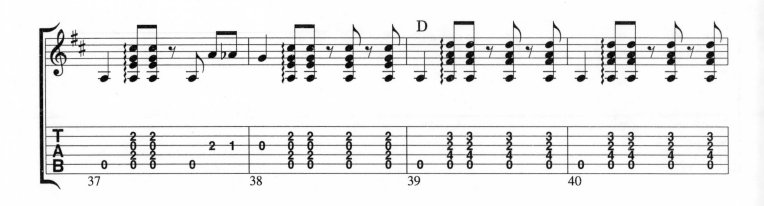

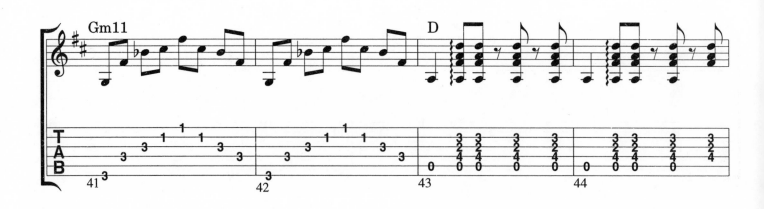

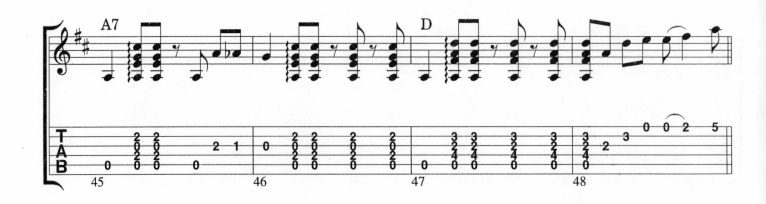

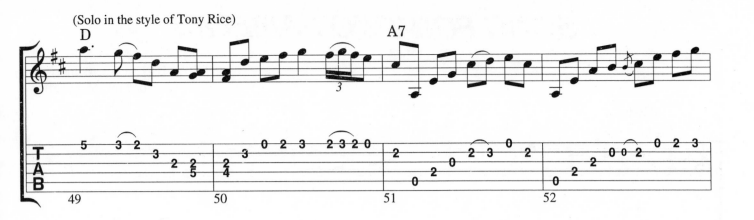
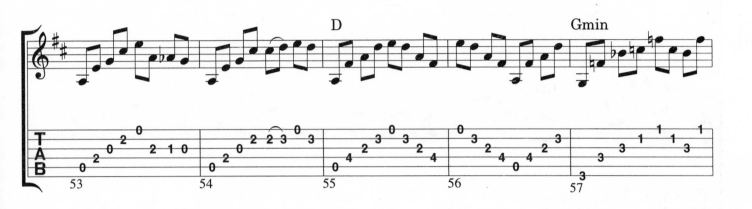

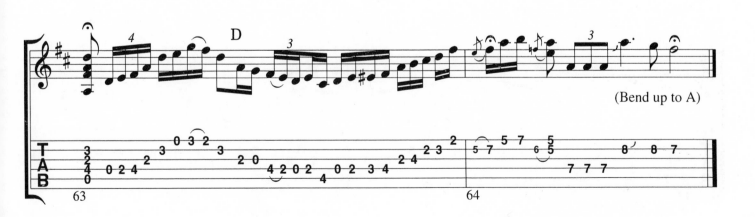

SONG FOR TWO PAMELAS

By David Grisman
Transcribed by John Carlini

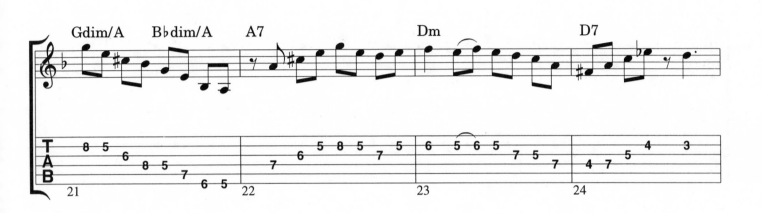

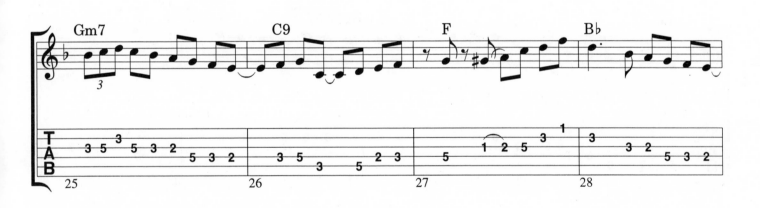

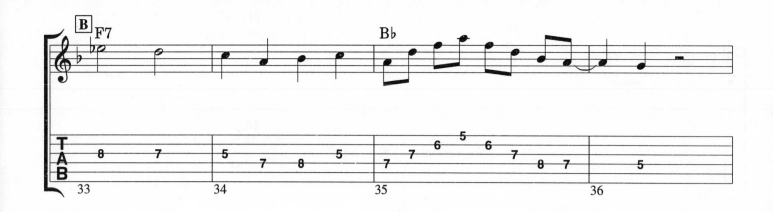

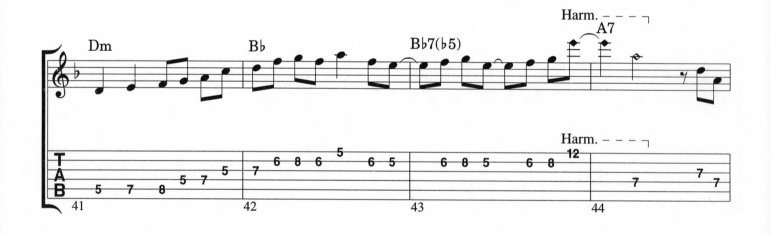

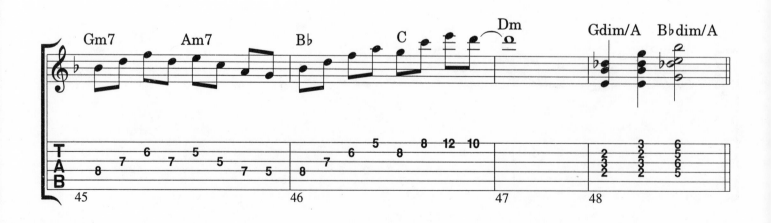

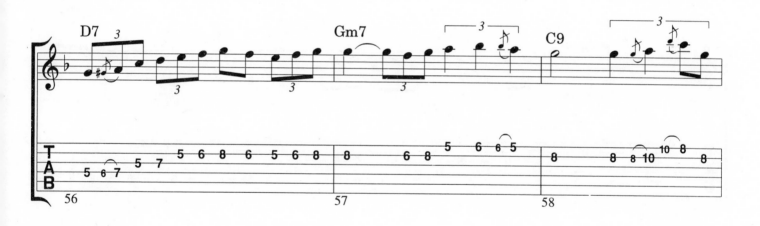

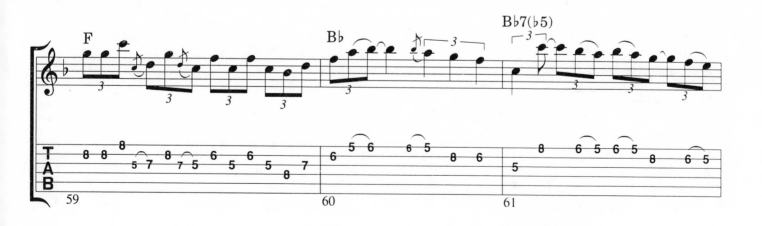

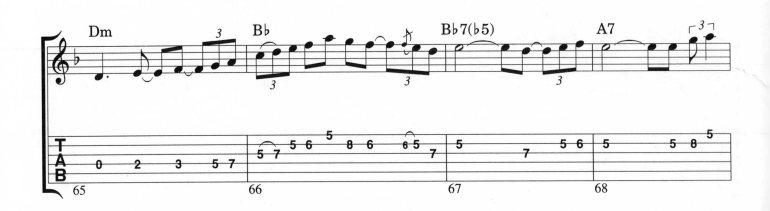

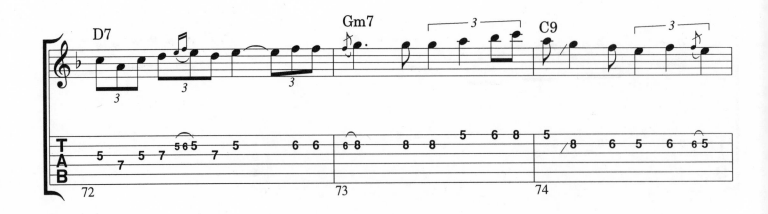

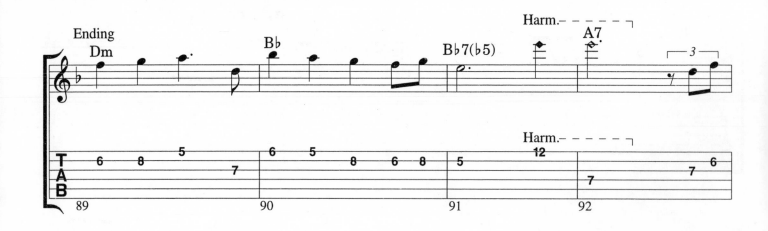

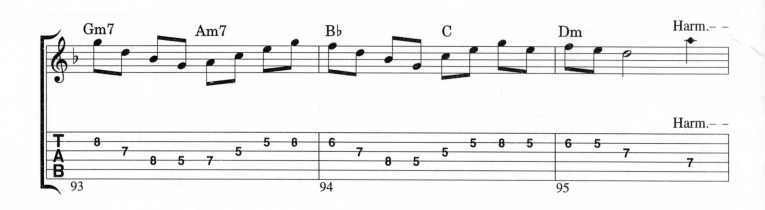

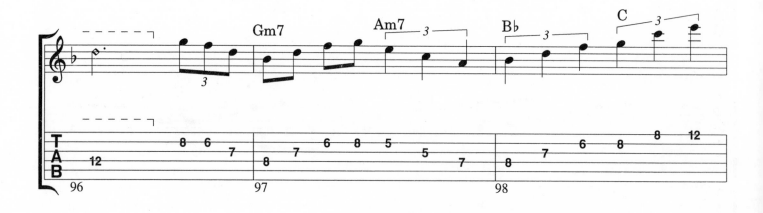

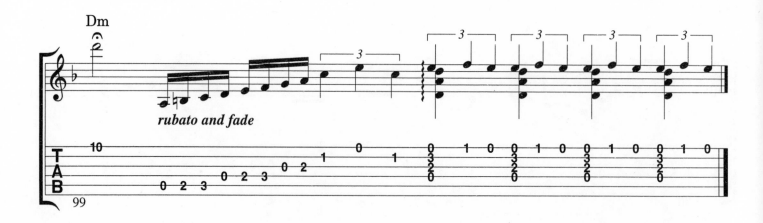